No. 1215
$10.95

44 WEEKEND PLASTIC PROJECTS YOU CAN MAKE

 TAB BOOKS Inc.

BLUE RIDGE SUMMIT, PA. 17214

FIRST EDITION

FIRST PRINTING

JANUARY—1981

Copyright © 1981 by TAB BOOKS Inc.

Printed in the United States of America

Library of Congress Cataloging in Publication Data

    44 weekend plastic projects you can make.

    Includes index.
    1. Plastics craft. I. Tab Books.
TT297.F68   1980   668.4   80-23607
ISBN 0-8306-9680-6
ISBN 0-8306-1215-7 (pbk.)

Contents

Preface

Plastics have come of age as worthwhile substances. They are materials compounded in the laboratory to have definite characteristics. Some plastics are hard while others are soft; some are rigid while others are flexible. Plastics are truly fascinating materials to work with.

This book describes numerous do-it-yourself projects that involve plastics. As a bonus, you get instructions for three additional projects, making a total of 47. Step-by-step directions tell how to make furnishings, candle and letter holders, decorations, molds, models, tools, toys and acrylic projects. There is a Chapter on various processes and techniques that are used in working with plastics.

All of the outstanding projects in this book have been made available by the editors of *School Shop* magazine, the how-to-do-it publication that has printed articles relating to industrial and technical education since 1941. Without their efforts and cooperation, this book would not be possible.

Furnishings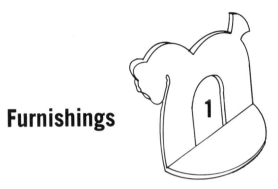

How about some plastic furnishings to spruce up your living quarters? This chapter explains how to make a paperweight, book ends, a place mat, vases, a hanging lamp and study carrels.

PAPERWEIGHT

Internally carved plastic cubes or paperweights are popular projects to make. Additional variety is achieved by mounting the block on an angular side and placing it on the base diagonally. The result is an attractive and unusual paperweight (Figs. 1-1 through 1-3).

Acrylic plastic 2″ thick is used for the block while the base is made of ½″ stock. The bottom piece for covering the carving in the block is opaque white stock (Fig. 1-4).

The block is cut on the band saw to rough shape and then sanded on the disc sander, which seems to work better than the belt sander on curves and angles such as those involved here. The surfaces are then smoothed with 3/0 emery cloth and, finally, with 8/0 wet garnet paper. If the surfaces are finely sanded, it takes much less buffing time to finish them.

Polishing is done on a buffing wheel with *Tripoli* compound and then on a clean wheel. The cemented surfaces are not buffed.

The flower and leaves are carved internally from the 1″ square surface. The design is a pansy with violet color streaked with yellow and white. You can produce the streaks of color by first putting in a little dye, usually the violet. Then partly fill the cavity

Fig. 1-1. This attractive acrylic paperweight will be a popular addition to a desk.

with plastic dust saved from the sander. By letting a few drops of yellow dye trickle into the hole more streaks of color can be produced. If a change in the color is necessary, it can be done by gently carving out the dyed portions.

Dry *plaster of paris* is then put in the carving, and it is moistened by letting a few drops of water fall on it. The leaves are then carved, using a separate entrance hole. The plaster of paris should be allowed to dry for at least 24 hours before the bottom of the block is covered. If this is not done, too much moisture might be trapped in the carvings.

The opaque white bottom piece is then cemented to the 1″ square surface of the block. This piece should be cut oversize.

Fig. 1-2. Note the internal carving.

Fig. 1-3. The convex surface of the face gives an attractive effect.

After it is on and the cement has thoroughly set, the edges can be sanded to perfectly match the 45° sides of the block. Polishing and mounting the block on the base finish the job.

BOOK ENDS

The design of these book ends makes it suitable for beginners and yet allows for originality as various animal or figure designs may be used (Fig. 1-5). The method of drawing full-size patterns on graph squares makes such a procedure practical. Variations in the

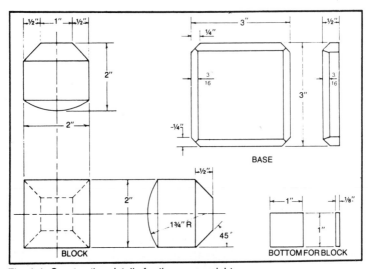

Fig. 1-4. Construction details for the paperweight.

Fig. 1-5. A simple functional design characterizes these plastic book ends (courtesy of Ford Motor Company).

design such as joining the two figures with a narrow rectangular piece make the project suitable as a napkin holder or letter holder.

Acrylic plastic is used because of the ease with which it may be worked, cemented and formed. This project gives excellent experience in choosing proper colors, laying out a pattern, sawing, filing, smoothing, buffing, polishing and cementing. The design is simple and functional and avoids the gaudiness of some plastic projects.

The construction steps for the project are as follows:

● Choose 3/16″ or ¼″ plastic in the color desires.

● Draw a pattern on graph squares and then trace on the masked covering of the plastic sheet (Fig. 1-6).

● Cut out the two figures with a jig saw or, if hand tools are used, with a jeweler's saw. Do not cut the base pieces until the ends are finished.

● File the edges and then carefully scrape with a knife or glass before sanding.

● Lay out and cut the base pieces to fit the width of the end pieces which may vary in size because of the scraping and sanding.

● File, scrape, sand and check the base piece for size.

● Remove just enough masking paper along the edges so that the cementing may be done.

● Make a cementing jig by fastening together two rectangular blocks that are slightly longer than the book ends. Be sure that these form a true right angle.

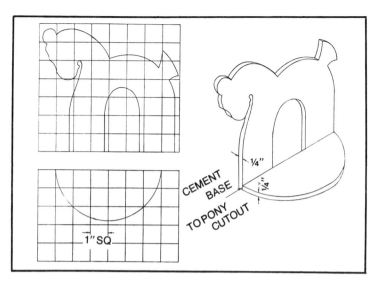

Fig. 1-6. Pattern for the plastic book ends.

● The cement may be applied with a small brush or the dipping method may be used. The softened surfaces are then pressed firmly together in the jig with wedges used for applying the pressure. Proper bonding is important, of course. Allow the cement to set overnight.

● Remove the masking paper, clean with a good cleaner, and then polish with plastic wax, using a soft lint-free cloth.

POLYETHYLENE SHEETING PLACE MAT

Figure 1-7 shows, with the exception of an oven, all that is necessary to make polyethylene sheeting place mats, lamp shades

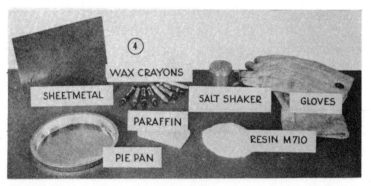

Fig. 1-7. Shown is all the material needed to make a polyethylene sheeting place mat.

and textured-surface sheet stock for room-divider screen. To make any of these items, obtain a sample of *Microthene M-710*, a piece of sheetmetal or a pie pan, wax crayons, paraffin blocks, a large salt shaker for applying the resin, and gloves for handling the hot metal.

Let us suppose that your initial experiment is a place mat. Using crayons, draw a colored design on the sheetmetal or in the pie pan. (The wax crayons become an integral part of the polyethylene mat.) You can make either a solid colored pattern with your crayons or you can use a line design. Next, any areas that have not been covered by crayon should be coated with the paraffin. machine or cooking oil.

Fill the shaker with M-710 resin, and sprinkle an even coating over all to an approximate thickness of 1/16″ to 1/32″. Remember, the plastic will stick to areas that are not covered with paraffin, machine oil or cooking oil.

Lift the metal carefully and place it in an oven that has been preheated to between 250° F. and 450° F. Place aluminum foil in the oven to protect the oven's inner surfaces from spilled plastic powder. In this heat, the polyethylene powders flow together and fuse, and the art work on the surface of the metal is absorbed into the plastic.

The plastic is fused in less than five minutes. Then remove it from the oven, and allow it to cool for another five minutes before removing it from the metal.

The result is a translucent picture which can be seen from both sides.

Various materials can be imbedded to add texture or unique designs in the finished item. For a variation, try the following. Paraffin coat the metal. Apply a thin coat of powder. Lay a piece of expanded metal on the coat. Apply additional powder. Remove the expanded-metal "stencil." Bake as previously directed.

LAMINATED BUD VASES

Projects constructed of plastic are not only functional, but interesting to look at and pleasing to the eye. You can make both small and tall vases. They are produced on a woodworking lathe, using ordinary woodworking tools.

Variations of "Sandwiching" Method

The two vases were glued up and laminated in two different methods. In Fig. 1-8 a series of colored plastics (reds, pinks, and

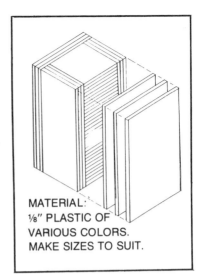

Fig. 1-8. Laminate procedure for a small vase.

MATERIAL:
⅛″ PLASTIC OF
VARIOUS COLORS.
MAKE SIZES TO SUIT.

whites), all of a ⅛″ thickness, are laminated on top of each other to the height which the maker desires. The adhesive used is *ethylene dichloride*. This can be applied in one of two ways. First, a small amount of it can be poured into a shallow dish. Then each piece of plastic is placed in the solution for about two minutes. They then are stacked on top of each other in the order the maker wishes. The second way is to use an ordinary medicine dropper to apply the adherent to each piece of plastic. Whichever method is used, when the two pieces of plastic are placed together, they should be moved in a circular motion to remove most of the air spots. The second method of applying the ethylene dichloride is a much neater way of applying the adhesive.

After this "sandwich" of plastic has dried, it can be sanded smooth by using a *disc sander*. Care should be taken in this operation to insure squareness of the plastic core at all times.

The next step is to glue some plastic vertically, the entire length of the laminated core. One piece of ⅛″ plastic and two pieces of ¼″ plastic are adhered to the four sides, beginning with the ⅛″ piece. When these pieces have set, the sanding operation is repeated, with care taken to keep the object square.

Alternate Procedure

In the second method of laminating, shown in Fig. 1-9, step 1, a piece of clear, 1″-square plastic 2½″ in length is used as the bottom core of the vase. This is pre-drilled with a ¾″ twist drill 2¼″ deep.

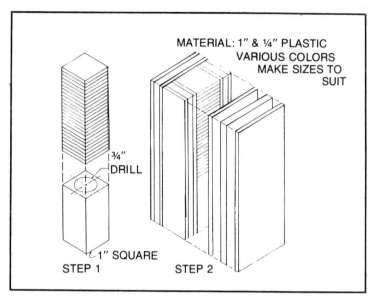

¾"
DRILL

1" SQUARE
STEP 1   STEP 2

Fig. 1-9. Laminate procedure for a tall vase.

The upper core of the project is made by cutting light green, dark green and yellow plastic of ⅛" thickness to a size of 1" square. These are then glued "sandwich style" on top of the 1" square of plastic covering the drilled hole. When this operation is completed and the pieces of plastic have set, the object is sanded with the disc sander, keeping in mind the squareness of the object.

The last step in the gluing operation shown in Fig. 1-9, step 2, is to apply some pieces of ⅛" light green and ¼" black plastic to the sides in a vertical position. Two pieces of the thinner thickness are applied, starting with the ⅛" material, and then alternating until they are all in place.

Cutting a groove from corner to corner, with the band saw, in both ends of the piece to be turned, is done to find the center of the object before placing it on the wood lathe. These grooves should be cut at least ⅛" deep. After carefully rough-turning the stock, the lathe can be set to a higher speed and the final contour turned by a series of very fine cuts. A round-nose chisel is used for the entire turning process; if it is sharpened frequently, there will be very little problem with the plastic chipping. The maker will notice that the tools which are ordinarily used in producing wood turnings on the wood lathe are also utilized in making the plastic projects described here.

When the turning is finished, the vases are sanded with 4/0 garnet paper, followed with grit 8/0 of the same finishing paper. To get a very smooth finish on the plastic and to remove all the scratches, *silicon carbide* paper with grits 400 and 600 are used. This finishing can be done either wet or dry. This sanding process, which is also done on the lathe, can be done at a faster speed than the turning of the object itself. The last operation on the lathe is apply a good grade of paste wax to add a finishing touch and enhance the colors of the plastic.

The last step in the construction of the bud vase is to drill a hole from the top to a desired depth for flowers. As noted above, the larger vase had the bottom portion of the core predrilled with a ¾"-diameter hole. Use the same size drill, start at the top, and continue drilling until you meet the hole that is already there. To determine the size hole to be placed in the other vase, find the smallest outside diameter and choose the size drill accordingly. All boring can be done on a drill press, run at a moderate speed while holding the project securely. The top portion of the hole may then be tapered outward by using a reamer. As a last step, the top and bottom may be sanded roughly on the disc sander, after which the garnet paper, silicon carbide paper, and paste wax are used to get the desired finish and shine.

MODERN HANGING LAMP

Having problems finding a project that will make good use of your scrap wood and plastic? This lamp fixture will do just that and at the same time give newcomers to woodworking the opportunity to express themselves creatively while developing basic skills (Fig. 1-10).

● Cut scrap plastic into random-size square and rectangular shapes.

● Cut ⅜" walnut or other suitable wood into random strips.

● Cut ½" walnut into 5" strips.

● Cut ¾" walnut into 14" strips.

● Construct the lamp's frame with eight of the ½" strips and four of the ¾" strips, using brads and glue. Size of frame can be altered to fit individual taste.

● Groove the ⅜" walnut strips in order to frame the plastic that was cut during the first step.

● Glue plastic in the frames.

● Arrange the framed plastic within the frame of the lamp fixture, filling in with random-size strips of wood; glue them in place. Handle the other sides the same way.

15

Fig. 1-10. This modern hanging lamp is made with scrap wood and plastic.

● Cut honeycomb plastic in accordance with the inside bottom dimensions of the fixture.

● Attach to the inside bottom a ¼″ wood edge to hold the honeycomb plastic. This way, the honeycomb plastic may be easily removed to replace a light bulb.

● Construct the top with ½″ walnut strips glued and nailed together.

● A ⅛″ hole is then drilled in the center of each side of the top frame to accommodate ⅛″ wire.

● Spray paint the chain and lamp cord in gold (we used 2/0 straight link coil chain and standard lamp cord).

● String ⅛″ wire through the holes and the last chain link.

● Weave the electric cord through the chain which has been cut to fit as needed.

● Attach a plug and light bulb socket to the lamp cord.

● Give an oil or similar finish to the completed project.

● Insert the top of the fixture.

Use the lamp either as a hanging fixture or suspended from a chain that drapes from the ceiling and follows along the wall to an

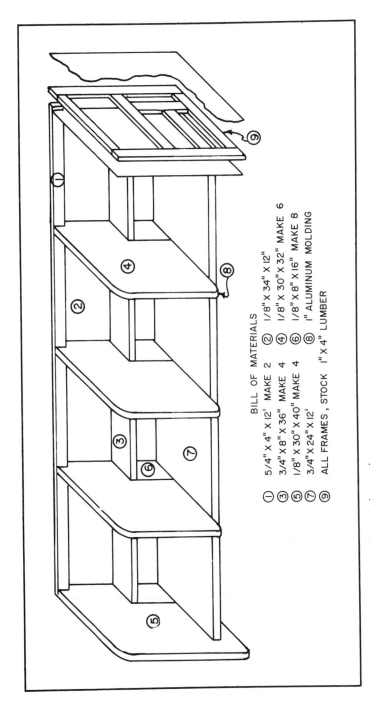

BILL OF MATERIALS

① 5/4" X 4" X 12' MAKE 2   ② 1/8" X 34" X 12"
③ 3/4" X 8" X 36" MAKE 4   ④ 1/8" X 30" X 32" MAKE 6
⑤ 1/8" X 30" X 40" MAKE 4   ⑥ 1/8" X 8" X 16" MAKE 8
⑦ 3/4" X 24" X 12'   ⑧ 1" ALUMINUM MOLDING
⑨ ALL FRAMES, STOCK   1" X 4" LUMBER

Fig. 1-11. Layout of materials for a study carrel.

electrical outlet. This is one way to use scrape wood and colorful plastic. And quite likely those scraps may enhance your living room order.

STUDY CARRELS

Study carrels are individual study areas or booths enclosed on the three sides. They are supplied by manufacturers of educational furniture in single units, or they may be bought in multiple units made up of two, three, or as many as eight carrels in a series. If you feel ambitious, you can make your own (Fig. 1-11).

Because of its low coefficient of expansion, *flakeboard* is used as a base material for all work surfaces to be covered with plastic laminate. The main work surface is made from ¾" flakeboard cut to a size of 24" × 144". Strips of flakeboard 4" wide are glued and nailed around the perimeter and over the joint.

The four individual shelves are cut from flakeboard and banded with ½"-thick white pine. The shelves, about 8" in width, are cut to fit between the carrel sides.

Different Colors

At this point the main work surface and the shelves are covered with plastic laminate. Use two different colors, covering the shelves with a beige and the work surface with an aqua laminate. Contact cement is used for the lamination A router is used to trim the excess laminate.

The two end panels and the three dividing panels are basically of the same construction, differing only in size. The end panels are made to extend below the work surface to improve the appearance of the unit and to facilitate attachment of support members.

These panels are made by constructing a framework out of stock 1" × 4" spruce lumber. Butt joints with corrugated nails and *polyvinyl acetate glue* are used in the construction of these frames. Particular attention is given to placing framing members in such a way as to allow later addition of wiring as well as the proper support of shelves and the panels themselves.

A covering for the panels is made from two materials. All dividing partitions are covered on both sides with ⅛" perforated hardboard. The end panels are covered on the inside surface with perforated hardboard and on the outside with solid hardboard.

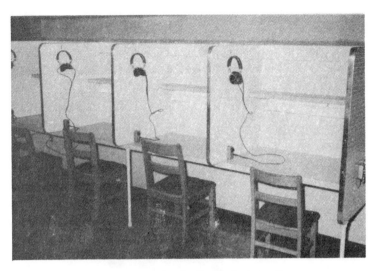

Fig. 1-12. View of a carrel unit showing the chairs in position.

Sound Absorption Is Important

One side of each panel is applied using contact cement, after which panels of a sound-deadening or absorbing material are cut to fit the space made by the 1″ × 4″ frame (Fig. 1-12). You might use *Homosote*, but any soft composition material such as acoustical tile can be used. These pieces are not fastened but merely secured by cementing the hardboard panels on the opposite sides. Any final trimming and rounding of corners on panels is done at this time.

Support of the *carrel* unit is gained by two methods. A band of white pine 5/4″ × 4″ is attached to the wall just under the work surface, and another of the same dimension is placed in notches at the top rear of the dividing and end panels. Three legs made from 1″ diameter pipe are placed under the front edge of the unit. The two outside legs are placed under the end panels and are necessarily shorter than the center leg.

The unit is preassembled using 3″ #12 roundhead brass screws to facilitate easy dismantling. The top band is attached with 2½″ #10 flathead steel screws.

After complete assembly, the unit is dismantled and all hardboard panels painted with a semigloss enamel. When the enamel is dry, the unit is reassembled, using the roundhead brass screws, and mounted to the wall—in this case a concrete block wall—with expansion shield and lag screws.

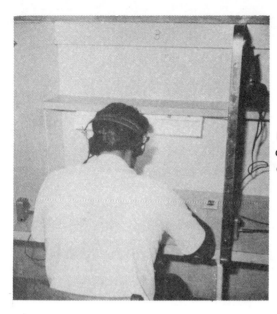

Fig. 1-13. A closeup of the interior of one carrel.

Added Touch: Light

Add anodized aluminum mouldings on the exposed edges of all partitions and end panels. To give the carrels total usability, you can add a 24″ flourescent light and a duplex outlet in each study area (Fig. 1-13).

Earphones are also installed in each booth and are wired to operate both individually or simultaneously. Individual volume controls with a plug-in jack are uses.

Holders 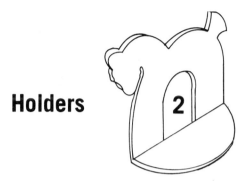 2

Here are some attractive and functional projects. All are relatively easy to construct.

PICTURE FRAME

This little plastic photograph holder involves many processes and uses of tools. The frame can be constructed with very little equipment. Variations can be worked into it such as variety in internal carving and dyeing of clear plastics, different sizes, colors, etc. (Fig. 2-1).

In order to get uniformity and balance in the finished frame, we use a mold to form it. This is cut out of 1″ stock as will be noted in Fig. 2-2. The mold may be parted if this seems desirable for ease in inserting and removing the hot strip plastic, although you can use a solid mold.

For the frame, use a strip of plastic 3/16″ × 1″ × 8⅞″. The ends are filed to remove the rough edges left by sawing, and it is then sanded with 4-0 and 7-0 garnet paper. After sanding it should be buffed on a wheel, using buffing compound, with final polishing on a clean buff.

The strip is then heated in an oven to 250°F. Remove plastic from the oven, using gloves to protect the hands and, before it hardens, quickly bend into the mold. When cool, remove it from the mold and lay out a ¼″ groove in each upper section to receive the glass. Cut it out with a coping saw and then put the picture between glass and assemble. Two pieces of glass 1/16″ thick, 3″ wide, and

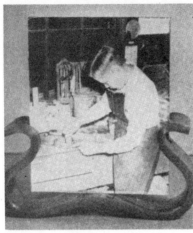

Fig. 2-1. This plastic frame can be varied in shape, size and coloring by internal carving and other methods.

4″ high will hold the picture nicely and complete an attractive looking picture frame for the home.

Plastics is an area in which there seems to be no bounds for creativeness and design (Fig. 2-3). The design for this pen holder and paperweight is simple. In making this project, you will use the band saw and do routing, handsanding and buffing operations. See Fig. 2-4.

Routing for the silver dollars is done on the drill press, using a ⅜″ router cutter. No template is used in this instance. For quantity production, however, a template can be used to advantage. Sand the routed areas with #400 wet or dry paper and buff with a small buffing wheel. The edges should be left sharp and true.

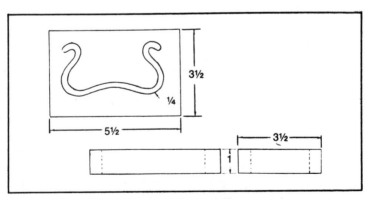

Fig. 2-2. The wooden mold is cut of 1-inch stock.

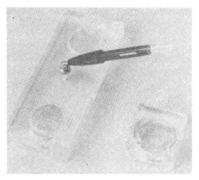

Fig. 2-3. It is not difficult to make this pen holder and paperweight (courtesy of Ford Motor Company).

Buff the dollars and press them into the depression, using just enough pressure to seat the dollars firmly into place. If too much pressure is applied, the plastic will craze around the edges.

Final sanding and polishing of the project should be done with care and accuracy. The beauty of the pieces depends on the sharpness of outline and brilliancy of clear plastic.

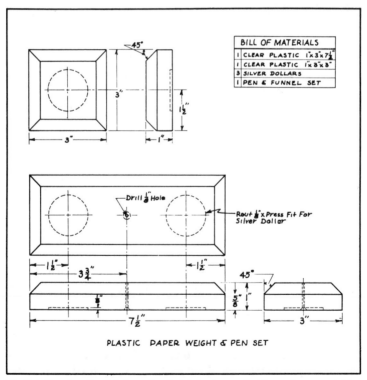

BILL OF MATERIALS	
1	CLEAR PLASTIC 1"x3"x7½"
1	CLEAR PLASTIC 1"x3"x3"
3	SILVER DOLLARS
1	PEN & FUNNEL SET

PLASTIC PAPER WEIGHT & PEN SET

Fig. 2-4. Construction details and materials for the pen holder and paperweight.

Fig. 2-5. The completed candle holder. Either clear or colored plastic can be used to make this attractive holder.

CANDLE HOLDER

Plastic ⅛″ thick, of the same color or of a combination of colors, can be used for this candle holder. This project is designed for an 8″ candle (Fig. 2-5). However, it could be scaled for a 6″ or 10″ candle. You will need the following pieces of plastic:

2—⅛″ × ½″ × 5″ for legs;
1—⅛″ × ½″ × 8″ for a handle;
1—⅛″ × 2¼″ × 2¼″ for a drip cup;
1—⅛″ × 2¼″ × 2¼″ for a candle holder;
1—¾″, 6-32 steel machine screw and nut. Some procedural suggestions follow.

Legs

Locate and drill the 9/64″ hole. Round four corners. File (using a smooth mill file), steel wool with 00 steel wool, and buff the edges. Remove masking paper and clean plastic. Heat and bend the legs in the leg bending jig (Fig. 2-6). Bend one top down a little so the legs will set level when crossed.

Handle

Locate and drill the 9/64″ hole. Round two corners. File, steel wool and buff. Remove masking paper and clean plastic. Heat and bend in the handle jig (Fig. 2-6).

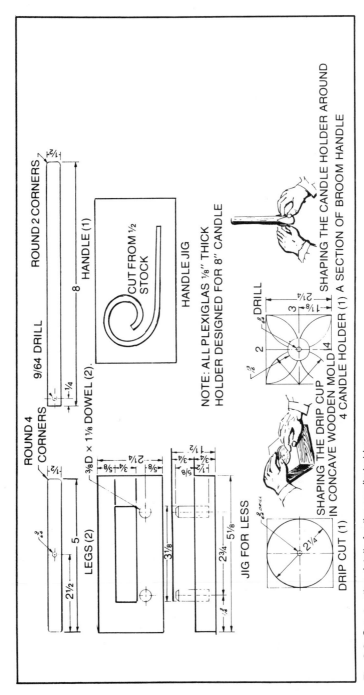

Fig. 2-6. Construction details for the candle holder.

25

Fig. 2-7. The finished clipboard has an emblem within the layers of fiber glass.

Drip Cup

Locate the center and draw a 2¼" circle with a compass. Drill a 9/64" hole. Cut out on a jig saw. File, steel wool, and buff edges. Remove masking paper and clean plastic. Heat and bend in a drip cup jig (Fig. 2-6).

Draw a 13/16" diameter circle with a compass. Locate four points and draw design with a compass. Drill a 9/64" hole. Cut out on a jig saw. File, steel wool and buff edges. Remove masking paper and clean the plastic. Heat and bend around a piece of broom handle or 1" dowel rod as shown (Fig. 2-6). Assemble with ¾", 6-32 steel machine screw and nut, with the nut on the bottom.

FIBER GLASS CLIPBOARD

Here are construction steps for making a fiber glass clipboard. See Fig. 2-7 and Table 2-1.

Table 2-1. Materials List for the Fiber Glass Clipboard.

Silk-screened cloth or other pictorial matter.
One piece of 2-oz. fiber glass mat, 12 by 18 inches.
Two pieces of 6-oz. fiber glass finish cloth, 12 by 18 inches.
Twelve oz. of polyester resin with catalyst.
Two pieces of .003-inch polyester film, 16 by 22 inches.
One clipboard clip, 6 inches, with two speedy rivets.
Mixing cups, stirring sticks, 1-inch brushes, acetone, masking tape, and an ink brayer.
Unit is approximately $1.75. Purchase clips and rivets from plastics supply company.

Fig. 2-8. This holder can be made of scrap material.

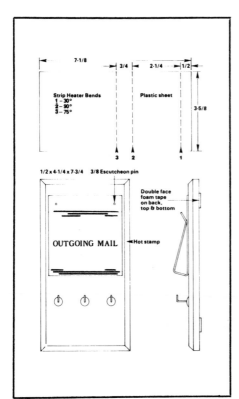

Fig. 2-9. Dimensions for the letter holder.

27

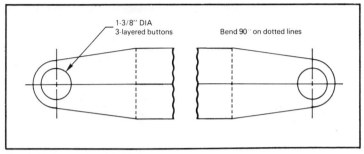

Fig. 2-10. Paper towel holder pattern.

● Tape a piece of polyester film to a smooth working surface. Mix 6 ounces of resin with 18 drops of catalyst. Brush about 2 ounces of the mixture on the film, taking care to stay about 2 inches from the edges.

● Lay on one piece of finish cloth and stipple with resin, working out from the center, until the cloth is saturated.

● Lay on some fiber glass mat and stipple with the rest of your first batch of resin. Don't over-saturate the mat or it will lose its strength.

● Mix another 6 ounces of resin. Lay on the design material face up, apply a small amount of resin and stipple.

● Lay on the second piece of finish cloth, apply the rest of the resin and stipple, taking care to work out all large air bubbles.

● Lay on the second layer of polyester film, carefully rolling out all air pockets with a rubber ink brayer.

● Clean your brush in acetone. Allow the fiber glass to cure overnight. The polyester film seals off the air and allows the resin to cure to a very high, hard gloss.

● After curing time, peel off the polyester. Draw the shape of the clipboard on the lamination and cut it out on a band saw (10 by 16 inches is a good size). Sand the edges lightly and apply a light coat of catalyzed resin to the edges. Allow overnight drying.

● Sand the edges and buff lightly on a buffing wheel. Lay out and drill holes for the clip. Fasten the clip with rivets.

WOOD AND PLASTIC LETTER HOLDER

Simple in design, this letter holder combines wood and plastic with a variety of tools and processes (Fig. 2-8). The wood base offers a challenge in design that involves either hand or power tools.

Fig. 2-11. The towel rack parts are being joined with solvent adhesive.

The holder can be made of scrap. The wood piece may be ⅜" or ½" stock. Availability and workability should determine the type of wood used. Poplar and black willow lend themselves well to either hand or machine operations. The plastic piece can be almost any type of sheet thermoplastic. If you desire clear or translucent material, acrylic or CAB (*cellulose acetate butyrate*) would be advisable. For texture and/or opaqueness, ABS (*acrylonitrile butadiene styrene*) or polystyrene will work well. See Fig. 2-9.

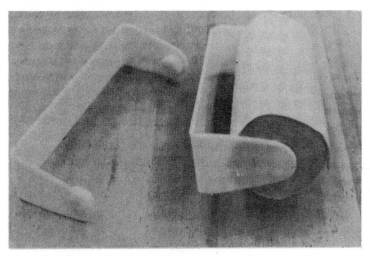

Fig. 2-12. This holder design is simple and functional.

This acrylic plastic paper towel holder design is perfect. It is strong, attractive, economical, functional and popular.

You need to trace and cut a pattern, cut plugs of plastic with the hole saw at the drill press, drill holes in rough blanks, and file, sand and buff edges (Fig. 2-10). Glue discs into three-layered buttons and shape the glued buttons into even cylinders on a belt sander. Finally, the shaped buttons are glued to the frame; the frames are then bent, using strip heaters to achieve the final shape (Figs. 2-11 and 2-12).

Decorations

3

If you are searching for some decorative ideas for your home, look no more. This chapter has two interesting suggestions.

PLASTER MOLD ORNAMENTS

Valuable learning experiences can be acquired in the construction of small plaster molds for slip casting. There need not be motivation only for large casting; some people prefer the tall and heavier vases.

You can construct the usual types; simple and multiple-piece drain or solid cast molds utilizing small or large models or samples. Differences manifest themselves in the weight of the plaster of paris used to prepare the mix to pour the mold sections, and in the amount of slip poured into the molds.

Ecologically, it is suggested that you consider the smaller models for mold making, precisely because there is need for less construction materials (i.e., plaster and slip). Subsequent savings in kiln space and firing schedules justify the financial rationale for promoting the casting of smaller projects.

You should be careful in the manner that you decorate small green or bisqued ware (Fig. 3-1). There is less surface area and usually less wall thickness. More care is exercised in manipulating the *fettling knife*, incising tools, and underglaze brushes, crayons or pencils.

Original models for the plaster molds are clay constructed on the wheel or at the bench. To facilitate the embedding of the model

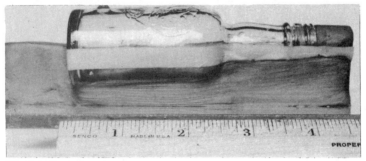

Fig. 3-1. Examples of green ware.

in the clay cradle up to its center line, you may use the conventional wax pencil to indicate the center or half of the model. Or use masking tape around the model and its clay reservoir (for the pouring hole). Build up the clay around the model up to the top line of the masking tape (Fig. 3-2). Then the plaster mix is poured as usual to obtain the first half-mold.

The small green or *bisqued* ware presents a most challenging situation. You can decorate the vases or figures with simple lines, using fundamental motifs found in nature: the scroll, circle, half-circle, two half-circles, zig-zag line, wavy line and straight line. If you prefer only to glaze the ware, use tongs to grasp the small projects when dipping into glaze. See Fig. 3-3.

FISH MOUNTING

Fish mounting, which preserves the appearance for display, is generally done by stretching the fish skin over a form representing its shape. The skin is treated for preservation, artificial eyes and jaw are added, and the display is painted. This process requires

Fig. 3-2. A glass model is embedded in a clay cradle up to the masking tape line prior to pouring.

Fig. 3-3. A plastic "floatie" and the casting, and a glass model with its clay casting built up.

time and skill to get satisfactory results. Special materials, not always readily available, must be purchased.

The fish is frozen in the desired pose, a two-piece plaster mold is made, the mold cavity is filled with resin, and the resulting plastic fish painted. Following painting, the mount can be fastened to a wood plaque. See Table 3-1 for materials.

● Freeze fish in desired pose (this is only to stiffen fish, so it does not have to be frozen solid).

● Construct wood or sheet metal form that allows at least 1″ clearance from all surfaces of the fish.

● Determine the plaster of paris needed to fill the mold slightly under half full.

Table 3-1. Materials Needed for Casting a 10-Inch Brook Trout.

Qty.	Description
3 lbs.	Pottery plaster or plaster of paris
1 pint	Clear casting resin or polyester resin used in fiberglassing boats
1 set	Model enamels or selected colors
1	Paint brush for fine work
1	Air brush
1	Small jar petroleum jelly
1	Quick setting epoxy glue
1	Piece of wood for plaque
Approximate cost of materials—$2.50	

- Mix the plaster by slaking it into water equal to one half the finished volume (hot water will speed up setting).
- When plaster begins to thicken, gently pour it into the form.
- Submerge half the frozen fish into the soft plaster.
- Once the plaster has set, carve locator pins in the plaster, and coat the exposed plaster with petroleum jelly or a similar parting agent (no parting agent is needed on the fish).
- Fill the remaining mold section with plaster.
- When the plaster has hardened, separate the two halves of the mold, remove the fish, and carve a sprue hole in the plaster. The sprue hole is usually located on the parting line of the mold. The fish may now be prepared for eating.
- Mix resin with hardener, and brush the mold cavity with a thin film of resin. Glass fibers, added where thin fins are located, will reinforce the resin (no parting agent is needed).
- Reassemble the mold halves, firmly secure them with rubber bands and fill the mold cavity with resin.
- After the resin has set, remove half of the mold. If the casting is good, it can be removed from the remaining half of the mold, but if fine details are missing, they should be touched up with epoxy glue before the casting is completely removed from the mold.
- Remove the fish from the mold, and remove the parting line and sprue (Fig. 3-4).

Fig. 3-4. Removed from the plaster mold, the fish is ready to be painted and mounted.

Fig. 3-5. This plastic molded fish is a good way to preserve the one that did not get away.

• Paint the fish (an air brush works best). Model enamels are fast drying. Put in details with an artist's paint brush. Oil paints give good results, but longer drying time is required to apply all the colors.

• Cut out and finish a wood plaque, and fasten the fish to it either by using epoxy glue or a machine screw threaded into the plastic (Fig. 3-5).

When fish over 1½ pounds are cast, cover the plaster mold cavities with fiber glass cloth and resin. This will produce a hollow casting which is lighter and requires less resin. Lay up each half of the mold separately, and assemble the two pieces using resin or epoxy glue.

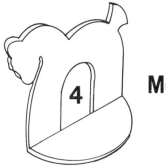

Molds

Many plastics projects require the making of a mold. This chapter discusses the construction of plaster and fiber glass molds. Another feature is the making of laminates with wooden matched-die molds.

MAKING A PLASTER MOLD

The first step in any project is its planning and design. Care must be taken in the initial design stages to provide enough draft on the part to facilitate its removal from the mold. If the part has undercuts or reverse curves, the mold will have to be made in two or more pieces.

The simplest mold is an open cavity made of conventional building plaster or special tooling plasters such as the United States Gypsum Company's *Hydrocal A-11* and *Ultrocal 30*. In the long run it pays to use tooling plaster because of its low expansion and great strength.

If it is necessary to make a mold of two or more pieces, cut a piece of *Masonite* to the shape of the pattern and place it on one side of the parting line. Use wood braces to prevent the parting line from shifting from the weight of the plaster. After the plaster has set, remove the Masonite. Coat the plaster parting line with a parting agent to prevent the second pour of plaster from sticking to the first. Pour the second half of the mold and strike off the excess plaster from the top of the mold box. When the second pour has set, take apart the mold box and

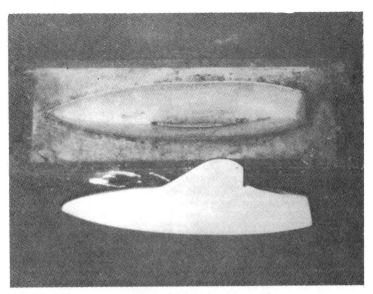

Fig. 4-1. A fiber glass sailboat model with a plaster mold.

separate the two halves of the mold. Break the sharp edges with a fettling knife or sandpaper to prevent chipping. Any defects in the molding surface can now be patched with fresh plaster.

The mold should be left to dry; the amount of time depends on its size and the humidity of the place where it is left. A small mold should be given at least two weeks.

To increase the longevity of the mold and improve the surface finish of molded hulls, the molding and parting surfaces should be given several coats of epoxy resin, after the mold is dry. Since the plastic is extremely porous, the surface becomes very strong and does not have any tendency to crack or flake off (Fig. 4-1).

MAKING A FIBER GLASS MOLD

Although more expensive and a little harder to make, a *fiber glass* mold is superior to a plaster one. With larger projects, it is impossible to move the plaster mold around; the plaster mold for a 50″ model sailboat weighs about 150 pounds whereas the fiber glass mold weighs only 15 pounds. A fiber glass mold can be repaired if damaged but the plaster mold will usually have to be replaced (Figs. 4-2 through 4-6).

A mold box is not necessary for making a fiber glass mold since the mold will be about ½″ thick. Apply a parting agent to

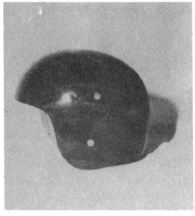

Fig. 4-2. Wood model for a crash helmet project.

the mold surfaces and edging. Then apply a gel coat of resin and hardener to all molding surfaces. After this has set, lay up layers of glass mat soaked in resin one at a time; do not attempt to build up the total thickness in one setting or the surface will crack. This procedure can be followed for a mold with one or more pieces.

With a large deep mold the resin and glass cloth tend to slide down the side of the mold. You can fabricate a metal rack from angle iron as a support for the mold and lay up the project half at a time without having the glass cloth separate from the sides of the mold.

In working with polyester resin, be sure to have adequate ventilation, and use disposable gloves, long aprons, and a polyethylene sheet over the bench on which you are working.

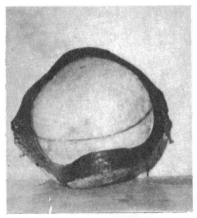

Fig. 4-3. Fiber glass mold for a crash helmet project.

Fig. 4-4. The finished helmet in plastic.

In order to remove a part from a mold, the mold surface must be waxed and polished prior to layup. Brush or spray on a thin coat of parting agent such as parting film of *polyvinyl alcohol* or wax. Wax requires a high polish on the mold surface.

The next step in the layup is the application of the gel coat to the mold to provide a smooth surface on the finished part. A

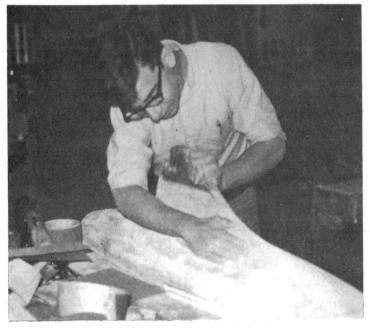

Fig. 4-5. Sanding the hull of a fiber glass boat with lead keel attached.

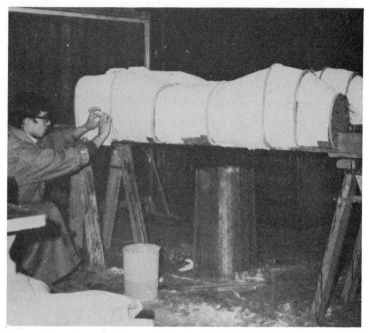

Fig. 4-6. Tooling up for a plastic go-cart—preparing the mold.

pigment can be added to the resin if color is desired. A polyester-type resin is recommended for the gel coat; it costs less and its hardening rate can be controlled more easily than that of epoxy. However, epoxy is stronger and has a less objectionable odor. Follow the manufacturer's instructions when adding the catalyst to the resin. Allow each layer to cure before applying the next layer (Fig. 4-7).

After the mold is coated with resin, apply the first layer of fiber glass cloth. Apply it in narrow strips to prevent it from bunching up; allow additional cloth to project out of the mold cavity to facilitate its removal. Use chopped glass fibers and resin mixture in places where the cloth cannot be applied or does not lie smoothly. Brush more resin on the fiber glass cloth till it is thoroughly saturated; use a rubber squeegee to work out air bubbles.

The second layer of cloth is laid up in the same manner except the weave is oriented at 45° to the first layer. Provide extra reinforcement for edges and sharp corners.

After the resin has set, the project may be removed from the mold. Since the part is not fully rigid, spring the hull away from the sides of the mold. Once the bond is broken, the hull may be pulled from the mold; a split mold must be disassembled in order to remove the part. Remove all traces of parting agent from the surface of the part. Repair minor defects with resin mixed with *thixotropic* powder.

WOODEN MOLDS AND PLASTIC LAMINATES

Making laminates with wooden matched-die molds is a project which will involve you in research, design and construction. The matched-die technique is used extensively in industry to produce fiber glass laminates. You can make undercut wooden molds to produce the laminates.

In designing the mold consideration is given to a minimum of 1° mold draft (required for the removal of the laminate from the mold), and the space between the male and female parts when the mold is closed (which determines the thickness of the laminate) (Fig. 4-8). Maple, due to its hardness, is the wood chosen for making the mold. It is cut to size and glued to obtain the correct thickness for the mold depth. The female part is

Fig. 4-7. Hand layup of a fiber glass project on a fiber glass mold.

Fig. 4-8. Undercut maple mold with the female part cut in half to facilitate removal of the laminate. Note the dowel pins in female parts.

turned on the lathe and the male part is turned to fit the female part.

The thickness of the cavity between these parts on closed molds depends on the stresses placed on the finished laminates. In this project, very little stress is applied—a cavity thickness of 1/16" is sufficient. This would be very thin, however, and would detract from the appearance of the laminate, so a cavity of ⅛" is allowed. This space is checked by the use of clay, when both parts are placed together.

The female part is cut in half to facilitate the removal of the laminate, since it contains an undercut. Wood dowel pins are used as guides for placing the two halves together. With the female parts of the mold together, the male and female parts are clamped by aligning the diameters of each. Then holes are drilled for the guide pins.

It is necessary for the surface of the mold to be smooth, since defects will spoil the finished product. After the mold is properly sanded, two coats of polyester resin are applied to the molding surfaces and between the halves of the female part. (The manufacturer's instructions should be followed when mixing the catalyst with the resin.) After the resin cures, the mold is coated with paste wax and allowed to dry. Then a liquid mold release is applied and permitted to dry. (Be sure to coat between the female halves to prevent them from adhering. If this step is not included, the laminate cannot be removed from the mold.)

Laminates made from the mold are all prepared in the same manner, with the exception of the decoration. Four pieces of fiber glass mat reinforcement are cut for the base of the mold, and three pieces of cloth reinforcement (because of its flexibility

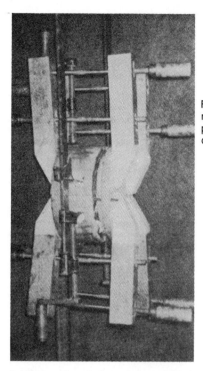

Fig. 4-9. Male and female parts of mold are clamped together and pressure is applied to the matched-die mold.

in fitting the shape of the mold) are cut for the upper portion. A sufficient amount of catalyst and the desired resin dye are mixed with the polyester resin. (It is better to have too much resin than not enough.) The reinforcement is placed in the mold piece-by-piece, after saturating each with resin. A brush is used to force out as many air bubbles as possible before closing the mold. Decoration is added to the last piece of cloth, or placed between the last two layers of cloth. Such things as chipped glass, fabric, color pigments, crayon, sequins, leaves, etc. are used.

Figure 4-9 shows how pressure is applied to hold the female parts together, and to hold the male and female parts in place.

Fig. 4-10. These are the attractive finished products.

The laminate is allowed to cure—usually from one to three hours—for one percent catalyst at a room temperature of 72°. After the curing, the male part is removed by taking out the guide pins and tapping the sides with a rubber mallet. The laminate is removed from the female part by separating the halves. Common woodworking tools are used to remove the trim and finish the edges of the laminate (Fig. 4-10).

Clothing Articles 5

The two items in this chapter can be worn with pride. Follow the instructions carefully.

LAPEL PIN

Music lovers will like this plastic lapel pin Fig. 5-1 . A number of basic operations in working plastics ar involved.

The pin is made from ¼" acrylic sheet plastic while the fingerboard is made from walnut. After the body of the violin is completed which involves sawing, filing, drilling, and polishing , the fingerboard can be made and the holes drilled for the brads slightly smaller than the brads themselves. The holes in the plastic should also be slightly smaller than the brads. The brads can be inserted with a *mandrel press* or with pliers protected with felt to prevent marring the plastic. Be sure to leave the two brads next to the bridge projecting enough to hold the wire strings.

Notches should be cut in the bridge and saddle to hold the strings firmly. Small wooden pegs can be made and inserted as shown in Fig. 5-2. The wooden parts should be shellacked. The finished pin is an inexpensive gift which requires careful craftsmanship to make and is appreciated especially by fiddle players.

BELT BUCKLES

The procedure for casting belt buckles is very interesting. Other cast products can be made this way, such as coins, wall plaques and desk signs.

45

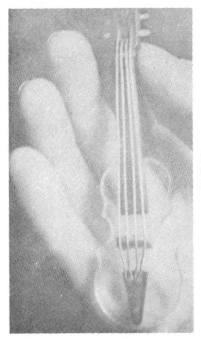

Fig. 5-1. This lapel pin is made from plastic and walnut and is an inexpensive gift for musicians.

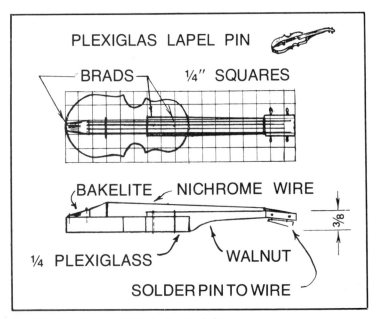

Fig. 5-2. Construction details for the lapel pin.

Fig. 5-3. The finished buckles are popular with youngsters.

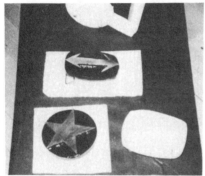

Making the Patterns

The first step is to buy or build a good hot-wire foam cutter. Next, develop buckle blanks, looking at actual buckles to get sizes. Cut a thick slab of foam the same shape as the buckle, and use the fence on the wire cutters to slice off blanks for as many buckles as needed. Also cut feeding sprues and runners from foam and assemble with white glue.

Buckles can be made to order, without remaking a major pattern. Another advantage is that large slabs of foam parts can be cut and sliced off as needed.

Casting

To cast, riddle about 2″ of sand into a flask, pack fairly firm, and shake in some setting sand. This allows for seating the patterns in the sand so that the bottoms come out. Then hand pack the flask to the top with sand, making sure the sprue is visible. Heat the melt a bit hotter than usual (about 1400° F) to make sure the foam flash burns ahead of the pour. Figure 5-3 shows finished buckles.

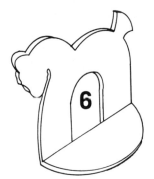

6 Models

Are you interested in model slot-car racing? How about architecture? If so, this chapter has two plastics projects that are yours for the making. Plus, you can build a plastic model indexing head.

SLOT-RACING CARS

Slot-car racing has become a large and blooming industry over the past few years. Most factory-made slot racers feature a deceptively simple looking chassis of formed aluminum sheet, cast magnesium or brass tubing, a small but powerful dc electric motor, appropriate gears, axles, wheels and tires, and a swinging pick-up arm and slot guide—all covered with a nicely detailed, but heavy, injection-molded plastic body, in a variety of scale sizes—mainly 1/87-(HO), 1/32 and 1/24. The bodies take the shape of every conceivable full-scale prototype race car or stock car.

Among slot-racing "pros," it is an acknowledged fact that a vacuum-formed "bubble" body is the ultimate in lightweight design. In response to the resultant demand, manufacturers now supply a large variety of "bubble" bodies, patterned after virtually every racing prototype now in existence.

To get going on this project, you need only a vacuum forming machine (we used a 7" × 7" unit), colored polystyrene or clear celluloid sheet plastic (about .020 thickness) and suitable molds. Mold design and construction can go two ways. Either way is fine, as the same amount of thought is involved.

Fig. 6-1. At the right is a commercial type body filled with plaster and ready for use as a mold. At the left is the vacuum formed body which resulted.

Mold Design/Construction Method No. 1.

The first method involves the sacrifice of an injection-molded model car body, preferably a well used body ready for retirement (Fig. 6-1). The car should be selectied with an eye open for undercuts and odd protrusions. Some undercutting is tolerable and many full scale racers feature such contours to aid in aerodynamics, so it is perhaps unavoidable. If you have undercuts, try to keep them on either the front *or* the back end. The sides are not so critical.

To start, remove any protruding details such as intake manifolds, roll bars, mirrors and exhaust pipes, as they will not mold. Next, having decided on which end will not be undercut, dam up the wheel openings and the undercut area with masking tape, working on the outside of the body, from its higher parts down to the bottom edge. Then invert the body, and fill it with a smooth mixture of plaster of paris. Level out the plaster, shake out any bubbles, and allow the works to set up; this is done to prevent the original body from collapsing under the heat and pressure of the forming process.

When the plaster has set, strip off the tape, sand the exposed plaster smooth, and cover any defects with plastic-wood filler or similar material. You might "engrave" the wheel openings and other important details by carving a thin line in the plaster right next to the plastic body.

49

Fig. 6-2. At the left is the pine body mold. In the center is the formed, untrimmed body. At the right is the finished body mounted on a racer chassis.

Mold Design/Construction Method No. 2

The second design method (Fig. 6-2) involves arriving at your own conception of the "world's best race car." Then get out your sketch pad, a bow compass and a straight edge. Draw a full-size view of the chassis, and then start sketching different body shapes until you reach you ideal. With a side view finished, sketch the top, front and rear view, also full-size.

Next comes the mold making. Pine lumber is probably the best all-around material, as it is easy to transfer the design to the wood and to shape the wood to the desired form. Wood finishes well, as it just needs sanding and waxing. If you contemplate making a number of bodies from the mold, a coat of fiber glass resin would aid durability, although bare waxed wood is pretty durable. You might consider using epoxy resin, plaster or perhaps even metal for a mold.

Whatever material you choose, however, make sure that the body is smooth. You will be surprised at the infinitesimal detail plastic will pick up from a mold, intentional or not. Desired detail, such as air scoop openings, metalglass divisions, door and wheel openings and trim lines can be lightly penciled on and then deepened slightly with a small Swiss file or knife blade.

At this point, you are nearly ready for forming. There remains only the drilling of small (1/32″) holes from the bottom of the mold to those areas which would become isolated from the vacuum source during the forming operation.

On to Other (and Bigger) Things

The forming process is simple and will not be covered here. The only precaution is to place the mold in the machine, on a diffusing pad, in a position which allows the maximum clearance between the edge of the machine and the mold.

After molding, the mold is carefully removed from the sheet of plastic, which is then trimmed to the desired outline, using a knife or scissors, and painted. Clear "bubble" bodies are painted on the inside, using special lacquer available for that purpose. Colored polystyrene bodies can be painted on the outside, using regular plastic paints. Add decals to suit.

There remains now only the mounting of the body, using tape, thin brass tubes and pins, or brackets and small bolts. Then, take the machine to the nearest track, where the competition awaits.

ARCHITECTURAL MODEL

Constructing an architectural model is often expensive and time-consuming. Here are some tips to help quicken the task and reduce the cost, using cellular thermoforming plastic sheet, an inexpensive material that is suited to demonstrating both traditional and modern forms of construction.

The cellular plastic comes on 40″ × 60″ sheets and is available from most art suppliers. Another way to keep costs down is to avoid specialty supply houses where possible and use model rail-

Fig. 6-3. Cut the cellular plastic with a frisket knife and straight edge.

Fig. 6-4. Assemble the model using white glue and straight pins.

roading construction material, which is available in two sizes: "O" gauge model railroad is ¼″ = 1′, and "HO" gauge is close to ⅛″ = 1′.

Begin constructing your model by fabricating the wall from the ¼″ thick cellular plastic covered with card stock on both faces. Cut the house sides and interior walls with a frisket knife and steel straight edge (Fig. 6-3). There is no need to make cutouts for windows or doors. Glue colored paper to the interior walls using spray contact cement, which is easy to apply, does not form lumps or stain, and allows parts to be moved easily if they are improperly positioned. Now glue windows and doors to the interior walls.

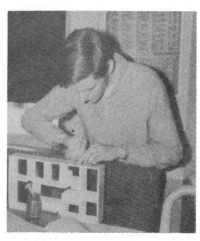

Fig. 6-5. Use spray adhesive to glue the wall covering sheets.

Avoid adhesives that will dissolve the plastic foam or embossed plastic sheet.

Assemble the house using white glue and straight pins (Fig.6-4). Apply printed sheets of building paper brick or siding with spray adhesive (Fig. 6-5). It is best to trim the sheets of building paper after the adhesive has set. Apply printed windows, doors, trim etc. in the same manner. Glue the roof together and hold it in place with pins so that it can be removed when desired (Fig. 6-6). You may wish to cover the roof with building papers or simulated shingles. Use a slab of 1″ polystyrene for the plot. The slab should be as large as the plot on which the house would be constructed. Use a surface forming file to "landscape" the plot, and apply trees, shrubs and grass as desired.

Add realism by covering the exterior surface of the model with embossed or vacuum formed sheet plastic using spray cement. The plastic sheets have a surface texture similar to the materials they represent. Injection molded windows, doors and trim may be solvent bonded to siding. Finally, paint the model.

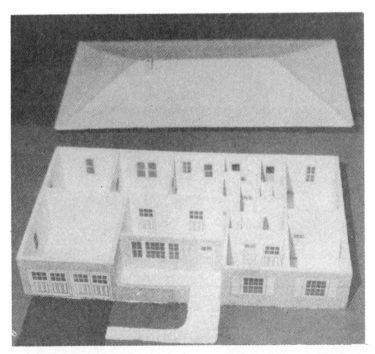

Fig. 6-6. The roof should be held in place with pins so that it can be easily removed to show the interior.

Fig. 6-7. This plastic indexing head is built from the manufacturer's blueprints and works in exactly the same manner as a standard head.

Fig. 6-8. Groups of colored parts are made out of colored plastic.

This exact reproduction of an indexing head contains 217 plastic parts and three metal springs. It was built from blueprint specifications supplied by the manufacturer (Fig. 6-7).

The plastic construction makes it possible to follow each step of the indexing process. To make distinguishable the essential working parts, plastic in different colors was used. (Fig. 6-8). The train of gears and shaft used for spiral cuts are green. The worm shaft, worm, and worm wheel are red. The spindle and the eccentric shaft are yellow. The center for the spindle is blue. All the other parts are clear plastic.

The helical gears, spur gears, *worm*, worm wheel, and housing were parts requiring high skill to make and intricate milling machine set-ups. Shafts, keyways, bearing races, and parts required many lathe operations. The work involved attention to close tolerances, of course, but did not utilize the milling machine. Dowel pins, bearing rollers, grease cups, and other small parts of simpler shapes were made.

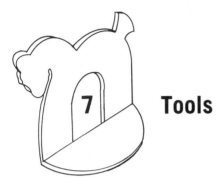

7 Tools

If you are in the market for some reliable tools, make a T-square and a set of screwdrivers with plastic handles. Both projects are relatively inexpensive.

T-SQUARE

The blade for this T-square is made of *methyl methacrylate* (Plexiglas or Lucite) 3/16" thick. A piece 12" × 24" is cut in six equal strips about 1⅞" × 24".

Bevels on the two edges of the blade are cut on the circular saw at a 15° angle. The saw table is provided with a maple insert. After this insert is cut to size and fitted into the table, the table is tilted to a 15° angle. The saw is then turned on and slowly raised to cut its own groove. This insert fits the saw blade so closely that there is no chance that the thin plastic will be able to slip down beside the blade.

Two feather boards, about 2" wide, are used to hold the plastic to the rip fence. The feather boards are made in this manner. Saw cuts are made in the end about 3/16" apart and about 5" long. The end is cut on an angle complementary to the angle that the feather boards are clamped on the saw table. The angle allows the plastic to slip along and the saw cuts make the ends of the boards springy. They will hold the plastic tightly to the rip fence and yet be flexible enough to allow the plastic to move freely. They are placed directly in front of and directly in

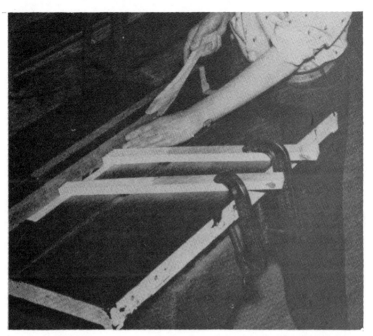

Fig. 7-1. Feather boards and a push stick are used when running a circular saw.

back of the saw blade. In addition to holding the plastic, the front board keeps the fingers of the left hand from moving into the saw. A push stick is used to avoid passing the hand too closely over the saw (Fig. 7-1).

These preparations may mean extra work, but they result in smoothly cut bevels. This saves much time later in the sanding operation. The insert and feather boards may be used on many other jobs as they are a safety measure when cutting thin material on a circular saw.

Plastic chips are hard and the force of their coming off the saw will wear a spot in the wood insert. Goggles should be worn to keep these chips out of the eyes.

After cutting, sand the bevels with a No. 0 garnet paper until the saw marks are removed. Be very careful to keep the bevel flat. A small sanding block used with 1/8 of a sheet of sandpaper is easiest to use. Then follow with a sanding of No. 3/0 to reduce the size of the scratches. Follow this with a No. 6/0 wet or dry garnet or a similar grade. Rub with water until all coarse sanding marks are removed. Lastly, as a final step, use a No. 8/0 metalite paper with water.

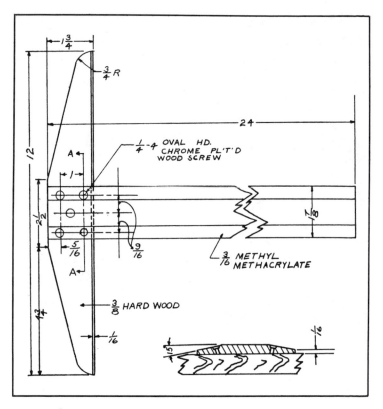

Fig. 7-2. Construction details for the T-square.

The plastic blade is now ready to be buffed. Use a *muslin* buffing wheel 20-ply section, 6″ to 8″ in diameter. Buff lightly the long way using a tripoli polish. Move the blade constantly to avoid heating and softening the plastic. If there are any scratches that do not buff out, the blade may be sanded again with the No. 6/0 and No. 8/0 and buffed again. The blade may now be prepared for assembly to any head from a commercial T-square using the same method of attaching as was used on the original.

If you wish, a head may be made from ⅜″ hardwood such as maple or walnut, as indicated in Fig. 7-2. A rubbed lacquer finish is attractive and durable. Use ½″-4 nickel-plated oval head screws in assembling. Turn in a steel screw first to thread the way and avoid marring the plated screw. Just before the T-square is assembled, it should be buffed on a clean wheel using jeweler's rouge. Wash clean with a mild soap and warm water and wax it.

Ordinary woodworking tools work well on plastic, but special sharpening is necessary for the best results. A hollow-ground circular saw blade, resharpened especially for plastics, will do. Edges of the T-square blade may be run on the jointer with a fine cut to straighten them. Do not joint wider surfaces of thin stock. Before boring, the drill should be reground to remove the rake. This will produce a scraping cut and prevent the drill from digging in. A counter-sink may be used without change.

SCREWDRIVER SET

A safe, attractive, and useful set of non-conducting plastic handle screwdrivers provides experience in bench work, lathe turning, forging, hardening and polishing. Standard drill rod and fluted plastic handle stock, available in colors from mail order houses, are the only materials needed. Plain round plastic stock can be ordered and fluted by indexing on a horizontal milling machine. Suggested dimensions for four popular sizes are given in Table 7-1.

Drill Rod Blade

● Use a large commercial screwdriver as a guide. All sizes are proportionate.

● Keep in mind that an imaginary line runs through the center of your work and that it should be forged evenly on both sides of that center line.

● Note that C is the widest part of the blade and that the distance between C and B is shorter than between C and D. Forge them the same distance apart and then draw file them to make C to D longer. See Fig. 7-3.

● Note that the width of A at the tip equals the diameter of the rod.

● Hammer one side at a time.

Table 7-1. Cut Stock to the Sizes Indicated.

BLADES (DRILL ROD)		HANDLES (FLUTED PLASTIC)	
DIA.	LENGTH	DIA.	LENGTH
¼	2¾	1	1¾
5/32 or 3/16	5	¾	3¼
7/32 or ¼	7	⅞	3½
5/16	9	1 or 1⅛	4

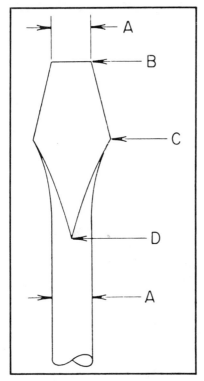

Fig. 7-3. Drill rod blade detail.

● Keep the piece red when forging and let the weight of a heavy hammer do the work. Be sure to hit squarely.

● Forge an extra 1/16 inch in all directions to allow for shaping the width and length.

● Don't grind and file metal away to get rid of dents. Instead, heat the piece red, place the dented side on the anvil and hammer on the opposite side.

● Grind draw the file to shape, and then polish the end so that color change will show. Harden to the proper color indicated on a hardness chart.

● Grind 1/16 inch chamfer on the handle for easy entry. Polish the entire blade.

Plastic Handle

● Hand saw in vise with protected jaws leaving 1/6 inch for facing.

● Mount and center work in four-jaw lathe chuck and face and chamfer handle end first.

60

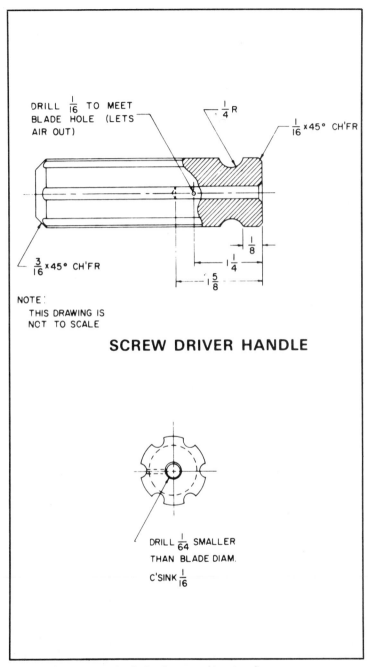

DRILL $\frac{1}{16}$ TO MEET
BLADE HOLE (LETS
AIR OUT)

$\frac{1}{4}$ R

$\frac{1}{16}$ x 45° CH'FR

$\frac{3}{16}$ x 45° CH'FR

$\frac{1}{8}$

$1\frac{1}{4}$

$1\frac{5}{8}$

NOTE :
   THIS DRAWING IS
   NOT TO SCALE

SCREW DRIVER HANDLE

DRILL $\frac{1}{64}$ SMALLER
THAN BLADE DIAM.

C'SINK $\frac{1}{16}$

Fig. 7-4. Construction details for the screwdriver handle.

- Chuck other end and repeat the second step.
- Cut 1/4 inch round groove.
- Drill blade hole—first with E-2 or #4 center drill—then drill a hole 1/64 inch smaller than the diameter of the blade itself (Fig. 7-4).
- Countersink hole 1/6 inch wider.
- Slide work out and hand drill 1/16 inch air relief hole in flute depression.
- When the blade is finished, support it at the tail stock and gradually force it into the handle. An alternate method is to start the blade while the handle is gripped in a vise with protected jaws. Use a lead hammer. Be sure to start it straight. The blade can be driven all the way in this way, or the work can be removed from the vise and held by the handle while hitting the handle with the lead hammer.

Toys 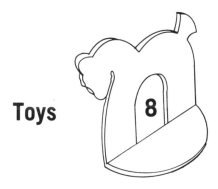 8

The finished items in this chapter will make nice playthings for youngsters. And you will get great pleasure and satisfaction out of constructing the toys.

PLEXIGLAS 3-D TIC-TAC-TOE

The basic tic-tac-toe pattern for this project has been changed from three positions to four. A third dimension, depth, has been added to the scoring possibilities. Now a player can score a victory by placing four of his colored marbles in a row on one plane, or by placing four marbles in a row on all four levels, vertically or diagonally (Fig. 8-1).

The game pattern is made on three 6″ × 6″ × ¼″ pieces of sheet Plexiglas and a wooden base. Sixteen indentations are made in each piece with a ½″ twist drill (Fig. 8-2). The three Plexiglas squares are supported by ½″ outside diameter Plexiglas tubing and ⅛″ threaded rod. Cap the threaded rod with acorn nuts and use hexagon nuts at the bottom of the base.

Cutting the Plexiglas

When cutting Plexiglas with a table saw, a 10″ 60-tooth general purpose saw may be used; a finer-tooth saw, however, will produce a smoother edge. Band saws, backsaws and hacksaws may also be used. A smooth cut can be obtained if the blade barely projects above the plastic, since maximum projection generally produces some chipping.

Fig. 8-1. Four-level scoring on a 3-D board adds interest in making this project.

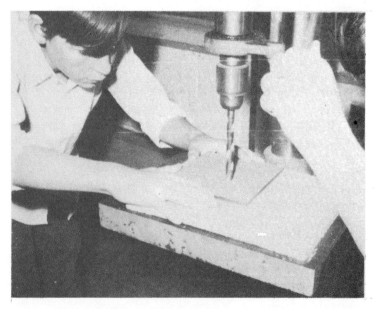

Fig. 8-2. Drilling the tic-tac-toe pattern is done easily with a drill press, setting the depth gauge to drill halfway through the Plexiglas.

Fig. 8-3. Mold parts and assembly mode, completed mold and the finished product.

Finishing the Plexiglas

Tool marks should be removed by sanding with a medium-grit (60-80) paper. To further improve the appearance, follow the initial finishing with "wet or dry" (150) grit paper. A transparent edge can be obtained if this is followed with grits to 400 and then buffed with a clean muslin wheel dressed with fine-grit buffing compound.

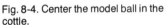

Fig. 8-4. Center the model ball in the cottle.

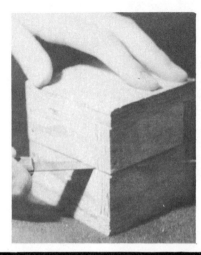

Fig. 8-5. Use a sharp knife to get a good parting line for the final pour.

POLYURETHANE FOAM GOLF BALL

Silicone and polyurethane are relatively expensive materials compared to polystyrene or polyethylene, but because this activity is small in physical size, the cost will not exceed a few dollars. The product is a soft, light, polyurethane foam practice golf ball that can be used as a toy (Fig. 8-3).

Materials for the project are a golf ball to serve as a model for the mold, ½" plywood for the cottle, nails, white glue, a scale for weighing the silicone, mold making silicone rubber (a 1 pound kit costs about $8.95 and will make about four molds), and flexible urethane foam of 4 pound density (a quart costs about $8.50).

Build the cottle in two halves so that the frame will split at the center line of the ball. Allow a ¼" clearance between the model ball and the sides, top and bottom of the cottle. Do not nail the top on at this point.

Suspend the model ball in the exact center of the cottle by driving a few nails through the sides of the cottle and only slightly into the ball (Fig. 8-4). Clamp the mold halves together, making certain the ball is centered. The top should be left off.

Weigh and mix the silicone and catalyst (about 130 g) according to manufacturer's instructions. Pour the well-mixed silicone into the cottle and nail the top in place. When the silicone is cured (the next day), carefully cut through to the model ball at the centerline. Use a sharp knife to insure that the parting line will seal well when the polyurethane is foamed in the mold (Fig. 8-5).

Drill a hole (about ⅛″) through the cottle into the mold cavity to allow air to escape while the polyurethane is foaming. A hinge or some other simple device will make it easier to line up the mold halves.

Mix enough foam (Part A with Part B according to the manufacturer's directions) to fill one-half of the mold cavity. The mold should then quickly be clamped shut as the polyurethane will begin foaming within 30 seconds from initial mixing. Keep the mold closed until the curing period is complete.

9 Potpourri

This chapter has a wide range of projects. Everything from a plastic gavel to an acrylic underwater camera housing is included.

GAVEL

In making the plastic gavel, attractive designs and multiple operations are combined to produce a useful and unique effect. The gavel head consists of seven pieces of plastic cemented together with a plastic solvent. Different combinations of colors may be used in building up the gavel head (Fig. 9-1).

Two pieces of ¾" Plexiglas are used for the faces of the head, and a flower design is internally carved in this face piece and appropriately dyed (Fig. 9-2). A black backing, glued to the carved piece on each end, reflects the colors in the carving. After all the pieces have been cemented together in a solid block, the head is placed in a four-jaw chuck and turned to a cylinder. Then it is shaped to the desired form.

The piece is polished in the lathe by using a very fine grade of sandpaper (no. 6/0 is recommended) and then finished with *pumice stone* and a damp cloth. After the piece has been polished on the lathe, it is buffed on a buffing wheel to give it a higher luster. A hole is drilled and tapped for the handle, with care being taken to get the hole drilled true.

The handle for the gavel may be glued up of several pieces, but a plain Plexiglas rod is very satisfactory. In turning the

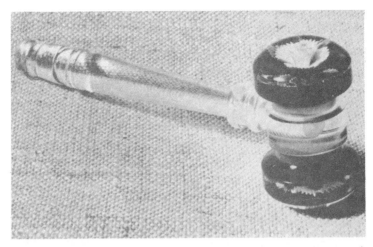

Fig. 9-1. Alternate layers of clear, black and fluorescent green plastic are used in making the head of this plastic gavel which has internally carved flowers in each end of the head for decorative purposes (courtesy of Ford Motor Company).

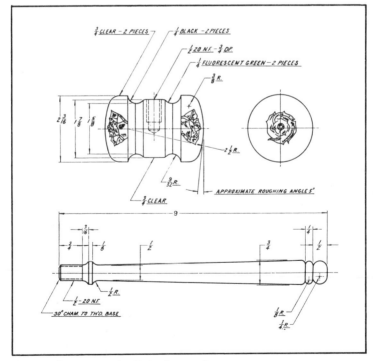

Fig. 9-2. Construction details for the gavel.

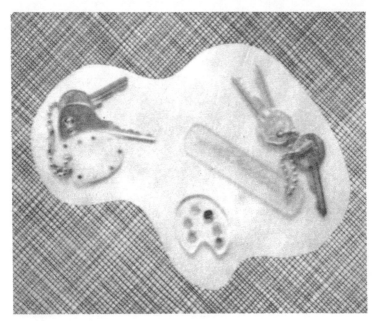
Fig. 9-3. The completed plastic key ring and name tag.

handle, the taper attachment on the lathe is used to get the proper taper. The threads are cut with a die, and these, too, must be true. The handle is polished the same as the head, using a file, fine sand paper and pumice stone, and finished on the buffing wheel.

In assembly, a solvent should not be used to hold the handle in the head. The solvent cracks the plastic at the thread base of the handle and causes it to break.

PLASTIC KEY RING AND NAME TAG

An interesting project using plastic is the illustrated name tag and key ring (Figs. 9-3 and 9-4). The key ring (shaped as an artist's palette) involves only one thickness of plastic.

Here are a few words about making the key ring. After the stock has been selected, the design laid out, cut out, filed and sanded, the holes should be drilled for the colored dots. Their size and depth is optional. It is best to use plastic dye, making certain, however, the holes are clean and dry. If plastic dyes are not available, regular coloring crayons can be substituted.

The tricky part about making the name tag—it can also be used as a key ring—is cementing two pieces of plastic together after the name is written into one piece of plastic using a vibrating tool or a wood burning set. It should be mentioned, too, that the inscribed name can be filled in with bright colored paint so that it will stand out through the second piece of plastic. Wipe off the excess paint.

To cement the two pieces together do the following. Put a very small amount of *ethylene dichloride* in a shallow pan, enough to merely wet the bottom of the piece of plastic, not immerse it. Make certain the ethylene dichloride does not touch the piece of plastic with paint on it. Allow the pieces of plastic to remain in the chemical for one to two minutes, or until the bottom becomes soft. Remove it from the ethylene dichloride and stick the two pieces together. Do not move the two pieces any more than is necessary.

To bond the two pieces, place them in a wood vise and tighten it until all of the air leaves the joint. A good rule of thumb—really, finger—is to tighten the vise "finger tight" and then take 1½ turns more. Remove your finger first, though! Allow the plastic to remain in the vise until completely dry for about 10 minutes.

The name tag can now be finished by cutting it to exact size, drilling the holes, sanding and polishing edges, and applying a coat of wax.

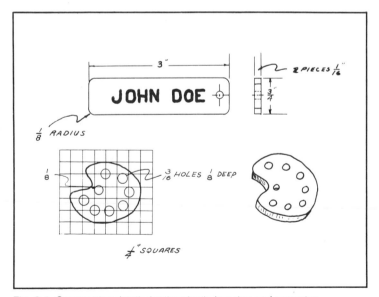

Fig. 9-4. Construction details for the plastic key ring and name tag.

APЬGDEHJKMNOP ＼STUVXYZ [

Fig. 9-5. Note that letters C, F, I, L and W have been omitted.

DRAFTING TEMPLATE

Lettering templates for drafting can easily be made with a 2D engraving machine. There are two basic types of drafting templates. The first, generally referred to as a *Leroy* type, consists of a piece of plastic with the letters engraved on the surface, and is used in conjunction with a three-point scriber. The second kind—a piece of plastic with the letters pierced through—is the kind you can make.

The template is first laid out so that all the letters of the alphabet can be produced. The letters B, Q, and R have to be engraved in two parts, while C, F, I, L and W can be omitted (as shown in Fig. 9-5). Once you obtain an optimum lettering layout, the type is set up in the engraving machine.

The templates are made from 3/32 or ⅛ inch acrylic sheet. A back-up piece is necessary, since the cutter is passing through the plastic rather than just engraving the top surface. The blank is cut in two passes with the engraving machine to prevent overloading of the machine's spindle.

After the letters have been machined in the blank, two thin plastic strips are solvent-bonded to the outside edges of the template. These strips raise the surface of the template from the paper and help to prevent smearing when the template is used.

Leroy, *Doric, Zepher* and other similar scales can also be made on the engraving machine. In order to produce the necessary slant of the letters, the ratio settings on the machine's arms have to be different. Settings for a given letter size must be determined by trial and error. The procedure for determining the ratios is as follows.

● Select the approximate reduction for desired letter height.

● Set four or five letter As in the engraving machine.

● Engrave the first A with the ratio settings equal.

● With one arm fixed, vary the ratio of the other arm until the proper lettering slant is achieved.

When the proper setting for each letter size is determined, it should be recorded so that the same results can be reproduced later. A fixed scriber of the Leroy type can also be constructed from plastic. A one-inch or larger Leroy or similar template can also be used to produce a set of smaller templates.

COOKIE CUTTER

If you have access to a plastic press, make this buffalo-shaped cookie cutter. High impact *polystyrene plastic* is the material used.

An experimental form is made of wood, which involves stretch and vacuum forming of the sheet plastic. The plastic sheets range in thickness from .06″ to .1″. One cutter is formed from the .1″ thickness.

A mold that will form four cutters at once is made. Wood is used for the buffalo patterns.

The plastic sheets of various colors and .1″ thick are cut into 10″ × 12″ pieces (Fig. 9-6). The cutters are formed in the plastic press, using the stretch and vacuum forming method. One hole is drilled in the cutter using the milling machine and a single end-mill cutter, 1″ in diameter.

The sheet is then cut into two parts on the woodcutting band saw. The cutters are then separated from the sheet on the

Fig. 9-6. Plastic sheets are cut into 10″ × 12″ pieces.

Fig. 9-7. The brass shutter-control rod is visible.

metal-cutting band saw. The cutters are trimmed and the sharp edges rounded off.

UNDERWATER CAMERA HOUSING

Constructing an acrylic plastic underwater camera housing can provide a valuable learning experience. In designing a housing that will enclose and allow operation of a particular camera for use in scuba diving or other underwater photography activities, you must allow for lever travel and control rods for two major functions of the camera—shutter manipulation and (in most cases) film advance (Fig. 9-7).

Cameras with a lever-type film advance are the easiest to plan for. An access for focusing must also be provided on most cameras.

Brass, ¼"-diameter rods attached to the camera controls and extending outside the housing can serve as controls for the encased camera. The rods can be secured where they pass through the housing by watertight, stainless-steel O-ring fittings. Attach a knob to the end of each rod.

A single-bend crank is used which depresses the shutter-control button when the knob outside is turned a fraction of a revolution. The film-advance lever is a double-bend crank; when its knob is turned, the lever is swung out, advancing the film. The spring return in the camera takes the crank back to its original position. The camera can be focused by a friction drive wheel, riding on the lens itself, turned by an outside knob.

Another major consideration for the case designer is the allowance for stops at places where the camera can be supported in the case. A force fit between the camera and the stops, made of the same plastic as the case, holds the camera in place. Put the lens of the camera rather close to the face of the case to reduce any distortion that may be caused by the plastic face. The use of the camera's view finder will be rather limited so you may want to put another view finder on top of the case.

Place an O-ring retainer on the inside of the back of the case. You can also put a stop on the back to lock the camera in position.

Construction

When the design for the housing is determined, you are ready to secure materials and begin construction. Six major pieces of plastic are needed. The ends, top and bottom are of ⅜″-thick clear acrylic plastic; the front face and back cover are of ½″-thick material. The height and width of each side are determined by the dimensions of the camera. Figures 9-8 through 9-10 indicate the detailed dimensions of the case that can be constructed.

The ends, top, and bottom of the housing are constructed into a unit first, with the ends placed inside the top and bottom.

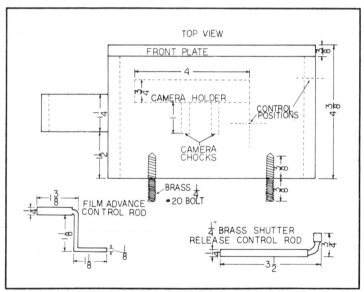

Fig. 9-8. This diagram shows the location of stops which lock the camera into the case, and of control rods which allow the camera to be operated through the housing.

The joints are cemented with ethylene dichloride which attacks the plastic and bonds or welds the joint together; this material can be secured from a plastics supply house. The two mating surfaces must be as true as possible to insure a perfect joint and a watertight case. When bonding the joints, soak the edge of one piece in a small puddle of the ethylene dichloride and then put it in place on the other piece. Be sure to work out all air bubbles caught in the joint. Soak the entire front edge of the assembled ends, top, and bottom of the housing in ethylene dichloride and then mate them to the face plate.

The back is attached with wing nuts on bolts mounted in the case so it can be opened for insertion and removal of the camera. The back must be sealed with a ⅛″ rubber O-ring stretched around a frame that will just fit the inside of the case. The diameter and circumference of the O-ring needed will be the same as those of the inside of the back. The O-rings and control fittings can be found at divers' shops or machinery-equipment supply houses.

The bolts used to mount the back are fastened to the outer edges of the top and bottom. You can use ¼-20 brass bolts for this. Drill the tap holes in the case and then tap them; be careful not to force the tap or it may crack the plastic. Install the bolts

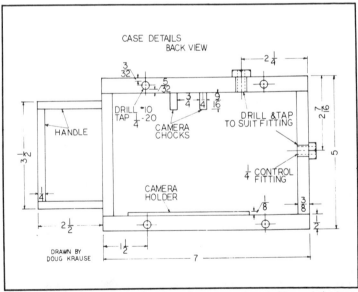

Fig. 9-9. Bolts to fasten the back plate on the case are inserted through the taps marked at the top of the drawing.

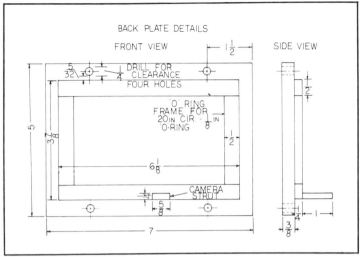

BACK PLATE DETAILS

FRONT VIEW — $1\frac{1}{2}$ — SIDE VIEW

DRILL FOR CLEARANCE
FOUR HOLES

$\frac{5}{32}$

$\frac{1}{4}$

O RING FRAME FOR
20 in CIR · $\frac{1}{8}$ in
O·RING

$\frac{1}{2}$

5

$3\frac{7}{8}$

$6\frac{1}{8}$

CAMERA STRUT

$\frac{1}{4}$ $\frac{5}{8}$

7

$\frac{2}{?}$

$\frac{3}{8}$

1

Fig. 9-10. Accented in this diagram is the proper location of the O-ring retaining frame on the inside of the back of the case.

and cut the heads off, leaving enough bolt to extend beyond the back plate and allow the wing nut to tighten down.

Installing Fittings and Controls

Next, cement the plastic stops in place and check for camera fit. The holes for the control fittings can then be drilled and threaded. The fittings are installed using silicone rubber as a sealant. Now the control rods can be constructed, installed and checked for proper operation.

You may want to install a handle on the housing and add a frame of colored plastic around the face to protect it from scratches if it is laid down on its front.

The amount of money saved in building this housing yourself is the best part. This case can be constructed for less than $10 and yet is comparable in quality and design to an $80 or $90 unit. This camera housing is a very valuable piece of equipment and can provide its owner with many hours of carefree use.

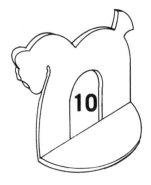

Plastic Processes
and Techniques

Various processes and techniques for working with plastics are detailed in this chapter. You will learn about the use of reinforced plastic, working with expandable polystyrene, surface pattern development, creative plastic embedding, blow molding, working with wood-plastic material, elastomer polymer technology, plastic sandwich construction, cementing acrylics and vacuum forming.

USING FIBER GLASS REINFORCED PLASTIC

Designing with fiber glass reinforced plastics is relatively simple. Keep in mind that this material has unique advantages and disadvantages. Your designs should utilize these characteristics and not necessarily follow rules for the use of conventional materials. Many parts can be integrated into one unit. Use streamlined or rounded shapes as they give greater strength than square corners and give a more pleasing appearance.

Fiber glass need not be built up to the thickness of conventional materials to give the necessary strength. Parts should be molded to shape and not "sprung" after they are molded. Fiber glass-reinforced plastics can be dyed to almost any color and may be transparent, translucent or opaque. Design to increase rigidity on larger objects, use maximum draft, and avoid undercuts in your designs.

Surface Treatment

Several types of surface treatment or finish have proven satisfactory. For a glossy finish you can sand the surface with #600

Table 10-1. Materials Used in Working With Fiber Glass.	Fiber glass cloth Fiber glass matt Woven roving Polyester resin Various color pigments Hardener Acetone Paste wax Mold release Lava soap Cabinet files Sandpaper (400 & 600 wet)

wet sandpaper and then buff with a soft wheel using hand-rub automotive rubbing compound. To provide a very attractive textured surface, you can pat the surface with a small sponge while it is curing or drying.

Another textured finish may be achieved, especially on transparent projects, by applying the resin rather thin so the weave of the fabric shows through the surface. One of the advantages of the materials is that color may be molded in and painting is not required. However, the surfaces may also be painted. Be sure all wax is removed and the surface is roughened by sanding. A primer should be applied, followed by one or two coats of paint.

Forming

The best way to begin construction of fiber glass projects is to use the contact method of forming. Alternate layers of polyester resin and fiber glass cloth are placed over a mold by hand lay-up. The mold holds the fiber glass materials as the project is laid up. Such materials as wood, plaster of paris, clay, metal and fiber glass make satisfactory molds. The mold must be constructed in such a way that the project can be removed when cured. Remember to use rounded corners, plenty of draft, and a minimum of undercuts or back draft. Table 10-1 lists materials used in working with fiber glass.

Projects made in a female mold are somewhat easier to remove from the mold as the material shrinks slightly when cured, and this tends to release the project from the mold. The smoothest side of the project will be the side that is next to the mold. To make a very durable mold, you can apply a layer of resin and fiber glass to become a part of the mold.

Your first project should be something similar to a round bowl or free-form dish. Then, after you get the feel of the materials,

Fig. 10-1. For a first fiber glass project, items such as bowls, trays and dishes in free-form are suggested.

graduate to planters, lampshades, knitting bowls, tables, chairs, etc (Figs. 10-1 through 10-4).

Place old newspapers over the bench tops and arrange your materials in the order in which you will use them. Remember, you do not have to be concerned about the resin setting up until the hardener has been added. Have a jar of acetone ready to place the brushes in immediately after using them.

Molding Operations

● Seal the surface of the mold and brush on mold release (water soluble) on mold.

● After mold release dries, wipe on two or three coats of paste wax.

● Cut the fiber glass cloth slightly oversize for the mold.

Fig. 10-2. Typical molds for making projects of fiber glass are made of wood, plaster and even fiber glass itself.

Fig. 10-3. Projects such as chairs, tables and other pieces of furniture are really challenging.

- Estimate the number of ounces of resin you think it will take to paint the mold and the cloth.
- Pour the resin into a jar or can. If the mold has steep sides, such as a lamp shade, you should add a thickener (a powder) so the resin will not "run."
- Add small amounts of color pigment if desired until you get the proper shade and stir thoroughly.

Fig. 10-4. Note the rounded design of these medium-sized projects. They are table tops, planters and lamp shades.

● Add hardener and stir thoroughly. Use ¼ teaspoon hardener per ounce of resin at about 70°F. If you find this sets up too fast, decrease the hardener. You will have about 15-25 minutes after adding the hardener until it is no longer workable.

● Brush resin on mold. Lay the cloth or other fiber glass material on the mold and work out all the air between the mold and the fiber glass. Make sure the fiber glass is in full contact with the mold.

● Apply more resin over fiber glass material. You may allow this mold to become tacky and apply more resin and fiber glass cloth or allow it to cure and continue at a later date.

● If the mold is allowed to dry overnight, file and sand the mold before applying more resin or resin and cloth.

● If you are working with printed fabrics and want the clear finish, omit the color pigments and thickener.

● If you get air bubbles or other defects, file them down, apply resin and fiber glass patch, and feather the edges when dry.

● The edges may be trimmed with aviation tin snips or cut on a jig or band saw. File or sand the edges on a disc sander. Apply your final finish coat of resin to the sanded surface.

● Avoid prolonged breathing of vapors. Avoid applying in a closed room. Use the same safety precautions for acetone and resins as you would lacquer thinner or other similar solvents. Do not store your resin in direct sunlight or near any type of heat. Do not allow it to freeze.

WORKING WITH EXPANDABLE POLYSTYRENE

Expandable polystyrene is used commercially for ice buckets, insulation of buildings, disposable drinking cups, floats for nets and a multitude of other products (Fig. 10-5). With a little work and practically no expenditure for equipment, you can start production. Material cost is low, and project possibilities are limited only by your creativeness.

The raw or virgin plastic beads are first carefully pre-expanded with a heat source. The mold is assembled and filled completely with pre-expanded beads. The filling hole is closed and the entire unit is exposed to heat, usually live steam. This further expands and softens the beads so that they fuse into the shape of the mold.

Fabricate a mold, usually two parts from cast or spun aluminum (Figs. 10-6 and 10-7). The surface finish on any part touching the beads should be smooth. Also, the usual principles of

Fig. 10-5. A few of the projects that can be made from expandable polystyrene.

Fig. 10-6. A drawing for a mold plus the mold and a planter made from it.

83

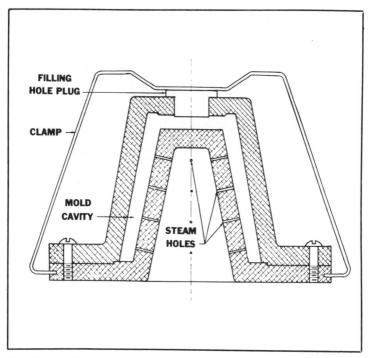

Fig. 10-7. A filling hole plug and clamp complete the unit.

draft must be observed to facilitate product removal. Small (1/32″) holes are drilled on the inside surface of the mold and one large (1″ to 2″) hole should be provided for filling. A "filling hole" plug and a device for clamping the parts together complete the unit.

Pre-expand the beads. Various methods are feasible. An endless belt (Fig. 10-8), moving slowly, and with a heat source above the moving beads will do a good job; or a shallow container with a layer of virgin beads may be placed under an inverted hot plate (Fig. 10-9). Careful observation is either case will determine the correct distance between the heat source and the beads and the proper length of "exposure" time. Should some of the beads come out of this step together, they can and should be separated by rolling them between your fingers.

Fill the mold cavity. A complete fill is necessary, and various mold cavity configurations will require different techniques. Gravity filling plus a little vibration will often suffice, but a vacuum source (portable shop exhaust systems) properly applied will facilitate matters (Fig. 10-10).

84

Expose to steam. Various methods of obtaining steam at 15-20 pounds pressure are possible; but a most convenient, simple and inexpensive device is a large pressure cooker with a pressure gage (Fig. 10-11).

Pour two cups of water into the cooker and place on a hot plate set to "high" heat. When the water boils, place the filled and clamped mold inside and tighten the cooker cover. After the pressure reaches 15 to 17 pounds, wait for about one minute.

Remove the entire unit from the hot plate, open the vent, and place under cold water. When steam pressure is "reversed." you will hear a sucking sound around the "safety plug." Remove the cover, take out the mold, unclamp, and remove the project. Air pressure through the mold "steam holes" sometimes helps remove the project.

A "large section" project will usually not "jell" completely through with the preceding method. A probe, constructed of ¼" copper tubing, having one end closed and with many small holes distributed over the surface, will then do the job. Develop 15-17

Fig. 10-8. A method of expanding the beads of polystyrene before pouring the mold.

Fig. 10-9. A container with a layer of virgin beads may be placed under an inverted hot plate.

pounds of steam pressure, force the probe into the filled mold cavity, and turn on the steam. Gradually withdraw the probe after one minute and then cool the mold.

If careful examination shows the project to be "perfect," the beads were correctly pre-expanded, the mold cavity was completely filled, the steam pressure was right, and the exposure time was correct. If the project is imperfect, one or more of the previously mentioned variables was probably not correct. Experimentation and experience will provide information to correct the fault.

SURFACE PATTERN DEVELOPMENT

The classification of technical drawing known as surface development can be described as representing those single curved

Fig. 10-10. The mold is poured with the aid of a portable shop exhaust system.

Fig. 10-11. An ordinary pressure cooker for steaming.

Fig. 10-12. An aluminum pyramid with plastic skin unfolded lets you see surface development in physical form.

surfaces that may be unfolded, unrolled or "flattened" onto a single plane. A surface development is likened to the peeled skin of a banana (or other common object) laid out flat on a smooth surface. To help make this concept of peeling a surface and flattening it more meaningful, a plasticized aluminum pyramid has proven useful (Fig. 10-12). Here is how to use the aid to understand this concept.

The seam location could be determined and cut as shown in Fig. 10-13. Peel the plastic as in Fig. 10-14. Complete the unfolding as shown in Figs 10-15 through 10-17. Lay the plastic flat and emphasize the edges with a felt marking pen to show the completed surface development, as in Figs. 10-18 and 10-19. While

Fig. 10-13. Unfolding begins by locating the seam and cutting.

88

Fig. 10-14. The front of the pyramid is unfolded first.

this pyramid shape works well, other shapes such as spheres, or even a banana shape, could be used with the plasticizing method.

The coating of metal items in industry has brought about the field of metal finishing. This process enables you to give problem materials, such as cast aluminum and cold rolled steel, professional type finishes. Plasticizing is also referred to as the *Whirlclad Coating System* and *Fusion Bond Process.*

Basically, the plasticizing process entails fluidizing some plastic or epoxy powder suspended in a cushion of filtered compressed air. The work piece is preheated and then dipped into the fluidizing powder. The coating is developed by the powder melting on the workpiece, thus forming a smooth and attractive finish. The piece is then cooled in water after the desired coating is gained. The coating thickness is controlled by temperature and length of

Fig. 10-15. The surface is unfolded from the front and one side.

Fig. 10-16. The plastic is removed from four sides and the top.

time the piece is exposed to the fluidizing powder. The plasticizing process works well on almost any shape of metal.

CREATIVE PLASTIC EMBEDDING

Instead of embedding by using purchased molds, why not try a method which incorporates an extra measure of creativity? You can attempt to create life like realism while transforming small snakes, insects, coins, pictures, or other desired objects into useful key chains, paperweights, bolo ties and science mounts (Fig. 10-20).

The secret to the success of this method is that all the embedding is done right-side up. The object is always in full view and there is no opportunity for air to be trapped under the object, which frequently happens when using molds.

Fig. 10-17. The unfolding process is complete.

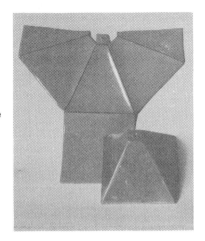

Fig. 10-18. Edges of plastic skin are accented with an ink marker.

Size Determines Method

You may choose one of two methods depending on the size of the object to be embedded.

If the object is less than 2″ in size, cut a piece of Plexiglas about 3″ square. Select a color of Plexiglas which complements the object, usually white for dark objects. Sand the edges of the Plexiglas with 80-grit sandpaper and position the object on the sheet of plastic.

Mix a small amount of casting resin with enough catalyst to ensure set-up in ½ hour or slightly less. Pour enough of this mixture over the object to hold it down when the resin sets up. Make a masking-tape box around the Plexiglas. Be sure to go

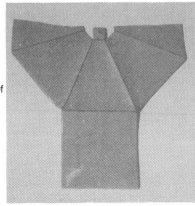

Fig. 10-19. Surface development of the pyramid is now complete.

91

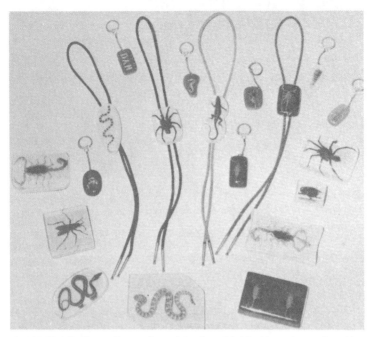

Fig. 10-20. Life-like realism and a variety of useful objects may be produced by creative embedding.

around twice and check to see that the tape adheres tightly to the base (Fig. 10-21).

Next, mix enough resin to cover the object by at least ¼″ and pour it over the object. Take a toothpick and remove all air bubbles clinging to the object. Don't worry about other bubbles; they will float to the surface and break.

Alternative Method

For larger items (larger than 2″ in size), the method changes slightly. First, cut a piece of Plexiglas larger than the object to be embedded. Remember that the size of the plastic will depend on what is to be made from the casting.

Second, adhere the object to the plastic with a quick-setting mixture of casting resin. When the object is secured, select a cardboard box into which the plastic will fit. The box must be deep enough to allow the object to be covered with casting resin. The corners of the box must be masked to prevent leakage (Fig 10-22). (Caution: The larger the object, the slower the object must be set up. Most formulas provided by manufacturers for mixing will work.)

The finishing process is the same for both methods. When the object is not sticky, cut it out to a rough shape on a band saw, file, and disc sand or drum sand to the final shape. The object is then hand-sanded, starting with 60-grit woodworking sandpaper and progressing to 600-grit wet or dry. Finally, it should be buffed until mirror-smooth.

Embalm Large Specimens

To prevent trapped body gas which could cause the object to explode when exposed to intense light, large specimens must be embalmed before embedding. The process is as follows.

First, inject the specimen with a 10 percent solution of *formaldehyde* using a *hypodermic syringe*. Position the specimen in a realistic shape and put in a refrigerator for 12 hours. This causes the specimen to become rigid.

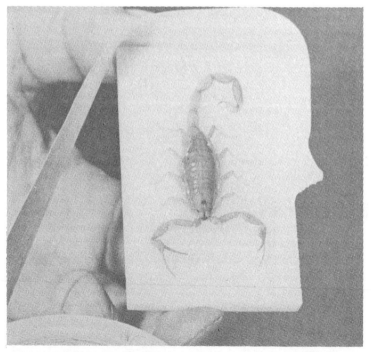

Fig. 10-21. Process for embedding small objects. A scorpion is secured to Plexiglas with a mixture of casting resin.

Fig. 10-22. Method for embedding large objects. The tarantula has a thin coat of fast setting resin poured over it.

Remove the specimen, wipe it off with alcohol, make a small incision on the underside, and take out all body organs. Fill the body cavity with a mixture of one part powdered alum to two parts borax. You may now proceed with embedding.

BLOW MOLDING

Blow molding is the process used in the production of the vast majority of hollow plastic objects. It ranks third, behind extrusion and injection molding, in total volume of all plastics material processed annually. It is the fastest, and generally the most economical, method of producing plastic containers and other hollow objects in large volume.

How it Began

The process of blow molding began in the early 1900s with an attempt to adapt the techniques of glass blowing to the new plastic

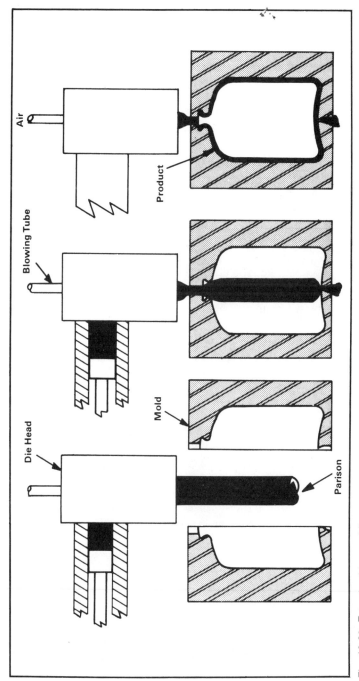

Fig. 10-23. Extrusion blow molding.

materials. The process of forcing air into the center of a molten glob of plastic was unsuccessful since, unlike glass, the plastic expanded unevenly.

Further progress was slow and limited until the development of better plastics and the perfection of the extrusion process, after which the present day process was established. In it, a heated plastic tube is formed, sealed at both ends inside a hollow mold, and inflated with air pressure to expand the plastic against the mold surfaces, where it cools into the desired form.

The blow molding process can be divided into two distinct operations: the formation of the hollow tube called the *parison*, and the inflating of that parison into the final form. The procedure for blowing or inflating the parison is consistent from one process to another. The formation of the parison, then, dictates the differences in methods and machinery.

The parison formation can be as simple as reheating a length of plastic tubing or using a hot, folded plastic sheet. But the more common practice involves forming the heated parison directly from the raw plastic material. Direct parison formation is divided into two categories which distinguish the two major present day blow molding methods, *extrusion* and *injection* blow molding. Each has its own advantages and applications.

How the Methods Work

Extrusion is the oldest and still the most widely used method of blow molding. In this process molten plastic is forced through an annular die, forming a molten plastic tube. This tube is then clamped in a mold which pinches the plastic together at both ends, creating an airtight seal. Forced air now enters the tube, either through a needle injected into the side of the parison or through a hollow mandrel in the die, causing the molten plastic to expand against the surfaces of the mold cavity where it cools and solidifies (Fig. 10-23).

Injection blow molding is a fairly new process which, although more complex, offers some distinct advantages over the extrusion method. Injection blow molding is a two-step process. The first stage involves injecting molten plastic into a heated preform mold around a hollow blow tube. The molten plastic is then removed from the preform mold by the blowing tube and placed inside a larger mold cavity. Air is then forced through the blowing tube, expanding the plastic against the mold surfaces (Fig. 10-24).

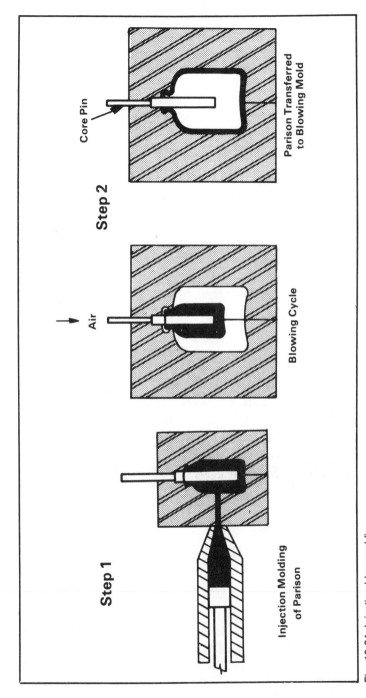

Step 2

Core Pin

Parison Transferred
to Blowing Mold

Air

Blowing Cycle

Step 1

Injection Molding
of Parison

Fig. 10-24. Injection blow molding.

97

The most important advantages of the injection blow molding process are the ability to control the wall thickness of the finished product and the freedom of finishing operations. Since it is a more involved process, however, injection blow molding is generally slower and thus more costly.

In addition to the greater speed of extrusion, further savings are possible because in this process several products can be formed from the same parison. Another advantage of extrusion blow molding is the need for only a single low-cost mold in contrast to the two molds required for injection blow molding, one of which is an expensive machined mold.

WORKING WITH WOOD-PLASTIC MATERIAL

Wood-plastic material (WPC) can be used for projects ranging in size from tiepins to tabletops (Fig. 10-25). Equipment needed costs less than $40.

WPC is produced by impregnating a water-like plastic monomer into the pores of the wood and then curing the monomer to form the plastic inside the wood by heating. Methyl methacrylate, known commercially as Plexiglas or Lucite in the polymerized form, is most often used because of its low toxicity and superior qualities, but *styrene monomer* can also be used.

The basic equipment consists of three tanks, an oven and an *aspirator*. The impregnation and surge tanks must be capable of holding a vacuum. A glavanized steel nipple capped on both ends and tapped so valves can be attached can serve as the impregnation tank. The surge tank can be wrapped with fine mesh window screen for added safety in case of implosion. It must be large enough to hold at least five times the volume of the monomer solution required to maintain a low vacuum once the monomer is introduced.

A satisfactory oven can be something as simple as a 3-½″ galvanized pipe wrapped with a 125 W roof deicing heating tape. The impregnated wood is placed in the pipe and capped with a rubber stopper, through which a thermometer is inserted into the oven.

Wood and Monomer Preparation

Only wood dried to 6 to 12 percent moisture content can be used. Soft maple, birch, aspen, cottonwood and basswood are preferred. Oak and black walnut should not be used because the plastic does not penetrate uniformly. The pattern of the piece should be roughed out before treatment to reduce waste of

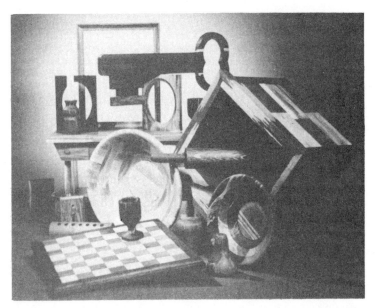

Fig. 10-25. Products ranging from planter boxes to tiepins are produced in wood-plastic impregnation technique.

monomer. However, reshaping after treatment is usually necessary because dimensional changes often occur during the curing step.

The solution consists of monomer, 0.2 percent *benzoyl peroxide* or *Vazo* solid catalyst, and 3 percent *ethylene glycol dimethacrylate* crosslinking agent. To add color, oil soluble dye must be used (1 percent of the solution).

Wood Impregnation and Curing

Refer to Fig. 10-26 to set up the impregnation equipment as explained below. Attach the aspirator to a water outlet having a minimum pressure of 20 lb/in^2. Plug the surge tank with a two-hole stopper. Insert a tube of some rigid material, such as plastic, into the left hole until it extends to the bottom of the surge tank. Insert another tube of rigid material into the right hole not more than 1" into the surge tank to insure that any water backup from the aspirator fills the surge tank, not the impregnation tank.

Connect thick-walled tubing, capable of supporting a vacuum, from the aspirator to the rigid tube in the left hole of the stopper and connect the rubber tubing from the impregnation tank to the rigid tube in the right hole. The rubber tubing connecting the impregnation tank to the monomer supply tank can be attached to the valve on the impregnation tank either before or after a vacuum is drawn; however, this tubing should extend to the bottom of the monomer supply tank.

Place the wood in the impregnation tank and weight it with a metal object so it doesn't float. Open the upper valve on the tank and close the lower valve. Turn on the water and let it run for about five minutes, which should be long enough to evacuate the air from the system. With the water on, isolate the aspirator by attaching a hose clamp to the rubber tubing connecting the aspirator to the surge tank. Then turn off the water.

Add enough monomer—by opening the lower valve—so that the level of the solution in the impregnation tank is at least 2″ above the wood pieces. Then close the valve. You will probably have to make a "dry run" in advance (using water) to determine the correct amount of monomer solution to add to the impregnation chamber. Remove the hose clamp so that atmospheric pressure can force the monomer into the wood for at least 30 minutes.

Open the tank (there is no danger from pressure release, etc.), and remove the wood workpiece from the solution, allowing the excess fluid to drain back into the tank. The unused solution should be stored in a refrigerator since its shelf life at room temperature is only a day or so once the catalyst has been added to the monomer.

Before placing the treated wood in the curing oven, tightly wrap the impregnated wood in aluminum foil and seal the folds with masking tape to reduce evaporation of the monomer. Concentrated monomer vapors are flammable; therefore, open-flame ovens or open heating elements should never be used to make WPC, and the curing process, using, for example, the oven suggested, should be conducted in a well-ventilated area.

Cure the impregnated wood in the oven for six hours at a temperature of 140 to 160°F. Using a deicing heating tape of the type illustrated in Figs. 10-27A and 10-27B, wrap the tape closely around the length of the oven as shown. Pre-heat the oven to the desired curing range before inserting the piece.

Making the Final Product

Wood-plastic material can be fastened, machined and finished much like wood. Any wood glue can be used to bond

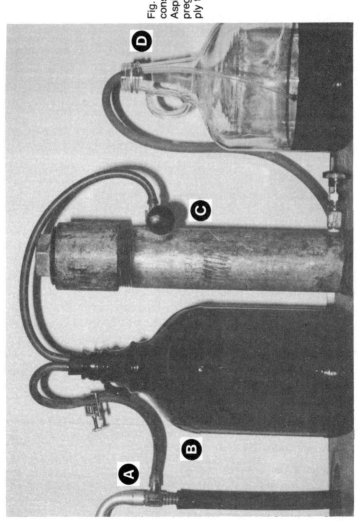

Fig. 10-26. Impregnation equipment consists of the following. (A) Water Aspirator. (B) Surge tank. (C) Impregnation tank. (D) Monomer supply tank.

101

wood pieces *before* treatment without damaging the glue bond. However, *after* treatment resorcinol or epoxy resins should be used. Polyvinyl, urea-formaldehyde or casein glues should not be used after treatment. Since WPC is harder and more dense than wood, carbide-tipped tools should be used whenever possible when machining it.

The material will split when nailed, so bolts or screws must be used to fasten the material. WPC pieces can be buffed to a high luster without using finishes, but oils and varnishes can be rubbed on surfaces to darken colors and increase luster.

ELASTOMER POLYMER TECHNOLOGY

Here's a polymer project that combines several concepts. The finished product is an exact replica of a commercial plaque or figurine. The activity incorporates the following materials and processes.

● **Development of an Elastomer (latex) Mold**. Latex rubber is one of the few natural polymers, and its use was historically important to the polymer industry. It is an inexpensive way to introduce a class to elastomers—material that stretches under low stress to at least twice its length and snaps back to the original length upon release of stress.

● **Reinforced Elastic Cottle**. The cottle which supports the latex mold is made from fiber glass-reinforced polyester. The part exerts great pressure when being formed, thereby demonstrating the material's strength.

● **Rigid Polyurethane Part**. The finished product is poured from parts A and B, which expand inside the latex mold and produce a dense, rigid mass. This process is analogous to that used in the woodworking industry to make furniture parts from polyurethane foam. The cost of polyurethane foam is high, but only a small quantity is required.

● **Moldmaking Techniques**. The three concepts above are amplified by the incorporation of moldmaking techniques. A related lesson in this area might be appropriate.

Preparing the Mold

In the first of the three processes involved in this activity, the product derived will be an exact duplicate (except for the finish) of the model selected. Models made of wood, glass, rubber and plastic have been successfully completed without

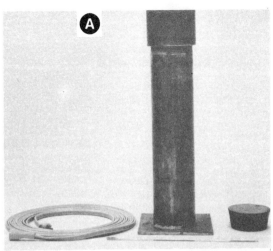

Fig. 10-27. A pipe oven for curing WPC. (A) Assembly of the oven parts. (B) The oven parts include heating tape, pipe, thermometer and rubber stopper.

using mold release. Porous models, such as those made of paper, need a mold release since the latex will penetrate the surface.

After selecting the model, use rubber cement to attach the model to a movable base such as polystyrene, polyethylene or laminated plastic scrap. Remember that negative draft or undercuts are of no concern with a latex mold.

Brush on 30 to 60 coats of room-curing latex (Fig. 10-28). Allow four to six hours between coats for curing time. Coat thickness increases rapidly after the first four or five brushings.

Fig. 10-28. Coat after coat of latex is applied to the model.

You can reduce curing time with heat from a desk lamp. Around the base of the model, brush a border of latex at least 2″ larger than the model in all directions.

After the mold has reached a thickness of 3/16″, it may be removed from the model. Thick molds have a much longer mold life, but it is sometimes difficult to remove thick molds from some models. Before removing the mold, add a thin film of liquid dish detergent to the outside of the mold to act as a lubricant while the latex slides over itself.

After the mold has been removed from the model, measure and record the liquid volume of the mold cavity.

The Foaming Process

To control the expansion of the urethane foam during the foaming process, make a shell of polyester resin, reinforced with fiber glass mat (Fig. 10-29). The model must be removed from the latex mold before the shell is added. If the latex will not support its own weight, fill it with paper towels or some other material that can be easily removed. After the mold is removed from the model and the film of detergent is still present, follow these steps.

Place the mold on a piece of polyethylene film and brush it with catalyzed polyester resin. The ratio of catalyst to resin should be determined by the speed at which you want to work. If you work for about one hour, a rule of thumb would be 10 to 15 drops per ounce.

After the mold is coated with resin, shred small pieces of fiber glass mat into the resin. Saturate each layer of mat as it is placed on the mold. Be sure to work out all air bubbles and work resin and mat over the circular base of the latex mold.

After shell thickness reaches ¼″ to ⅜″, allow it to cure thoroughly. After curing, remove the mold by pulling it out.

Cut the polyester shell in as many pieces as necessary to enable removing the shell from the mold after the reproduction has been foamed. Shell pieces may be held in place during the foaming process by hose clamps, vise, or both. A vise is best for holding the shell and mold since this frees both hands and prevents spillage.

Drill the polyester shell pieces and a scrap of wood to act as the base of the cavity. Prepare bolts of appropriate size to secure the polyester shell to the wood base.

Fasten a scrap of polyethylene (from a milk bottle) to the wood base, and before each foaming process apply a liberal coat of mold release.

At this point, the amount of foam required (equal to half the mold volume) can be calculated and prepared. To determine the amount of base and blowing agent to use, mix 25 percent of the total mold volume of part A with 25 percent of the mold volume of part B.

Example: mold cavity = 100 ml.
    50 percent mold cavity = 50 ml.
    25 percent mold cavity = 25 ml.

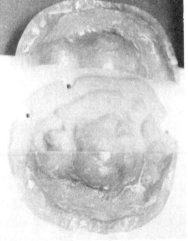

Fig. 10-29. A reinforced polyester shell controls the expansion of the foam.

105

Fig. 10-30. The urethane foam is quickly poured into the mold cavity.

Urethane foam mixture:
    monomer (Part A) = 25 ml.
    blowing agent (Part B) = 25 ml.

Follow manufacturer's directions for foam mixing. Quickly pour equal parts of A and B together in a third container and mix rapidly and thoroughly. The mixture will begin foaming in about 30 seconds. Pour into mold cavity and quickly attach base, being sure to allow the trapped air to escape (Fig. 10-30). Demold characteristics are usually 10 minutes for each 1-½" of cross-sectional height. See Figs. 10-31 through 10-33.

Fig. 10-31. A sliding entry sprue hole in the wooden base is optional.

Fig. 10-32. The model, mold and reinforced shell represent different stages in the process.

PLASTIC SANDWICH CONSTRUCTION

Sandwich construction literally "sandwiches" a core material of low specific gravity, such as styrofoam, between two layers of high strength facings, such as fiber glass. The core material may be cellular plastic, honeycomb or any similar material. This composite structure has tremendous advantages over other forms of construction when comparing the stiffness/ weight ratio. The tensile strength and bending strength are determined by the facing materials and the thickness of the core determines the stiffness of the sandwich.

The example of sandwich construction which most people are familiar with is the *surfboard* (Fig. 10-34). A number of small boats and surfboards have been made with sandwich construction techniques.

Many shop-built fiber glass boats are plagued with cracking problems. This is primarily the result of lack of stiffness which is provided by foam in sandwich construction. Foam in many cases was used strictly for flotation without consideration of its structural properties. When foam is properly utilized in sandwich construction, the cracking problems disappear.

The additional stiffness obtained by using sandwich construction is very easy to demonstrate. Use two samples: a piece of laminated fiber glass using four 2″ × 36″ layers of cloth, and a

Fig. 10-33. A finished product is shown with its mold.

Fig. 10-34. Sanding a styrofoam surfboard blank.

composite structure using faces made of two layers of fiber glass bonded to a ¼" plyfoam (PVC) core. Both samples are supported at their ends and a weight is placed on the center of each sample. You will be amazed at the additional stiffness that the cellular plastic core adds to the composite structure.

Rigid cellular plastic may be purchased in logs, slabs, and sheets of foamed plastics such as styrofoam, urethane and polyvinyl chloride (PVC). It may also be purchased in a two or more part liquid system such as *urethane*.

Urethane System

Polyurethane as used in some commercial applications is usually purchased in a two-part system which requires only the mixing (by machine or by hand) of equal volumes to produce the rigid foam. The basic urethane system contains the basic resin, a catalyst, a blowing agent and cell stabilizers. In industrial application the amounts of the individual components of the system are carefully controlled. This allows the manufacturer to control the chemical and mechanical properties as well as the density (from 1 to 70 pound/cubic feet) of the material.

The molds which you can use for hand layup of fiber glass are also used when casting parts of urethane foam. It is possible to cast solid as well as thin wall parts in these molds. A parting agent must be applied to the surface of the mold to prevent the foam from sticking. When mixing urethane ingredients for solid cast parts, it is best to mix them in paper cups or tin cans and discard after use. Cover the work area with a polyethylene drop cloth, and wear throw-away plastic gloves. A drill with a paint stirrer will do a thorough job of mixing. Pour the foaming plastic into the mold and clamp the top of the mold in place. The top of the mold should have a hole in it to allow the excess foam to escape. After the foam has cured, the part may be removed from the mold.

Spraying-Up Urethane

It is also possible to spray up foam and produce a thin-walled structure (Fig. 10-35). There are several industrial machines which are available for this, but their cost is usually prohibitive. There is, however, a low cost unit for spray-up of foamed urethane—the "Insta Foam Froth Pak." This is basically

Fig. 10-35. Spraying up urethane foam plastic in a sailboat mold.

a throw-away foam machine that comes in 1, 10, 25 and 50 cubic foot sizes. Insta Froth Pak is a dual system where the "A" and "B" urethane ingredients are in separate pressurized cans. When the valve is released (both cans valves are coupled), the two components mix and foam through a common spray nozzle. There is virtually no waste since you can stop foaming by shutting off the valve. The cost is very competitive with mix-and-pour systems, and is much cleaner (Fig. 10-36).

Foam spray-up can also be demonstrated by mixing the "A" and "B" components in a plastic squeeze bottle. The spout of these polyethylene bottles can be reshaped using a hot metal screwdriver blade to produce a fan shape at the nozzle.

With a little practice, it is easy to control the thickness of the foam being sprayed-up in the mold. The rate at which you move the nozzle will determine the thickness of foam applied. If greater thickness is required, you can go back and deposit more foam over the first layer of foam. After the foam has set, any irregularities may be sanded away. While curing time will vary with formulation, it is best to leave it for 24 hours so that the foam may obtain maximum strength.

Polyvinyl Chloride

Increased stiffness is not the only advantage obtained by using PVC sandwich construction. PVC foam is resilient and dampens the vibrations which could lead to fatigue cracking. The foam may be compressed to approximately one-half its thickness without any permanent damage to its cell structure; hence, small local impacts tend to be absorbed without doing damage.

Since PVC foam is a thermoplastic, it must be heated to form compound curves. The foam sheet becomes quite pliable at about 200°F. Small localized areas can be readily worked with a sun lamp, but large areas require that the whole sheet be heated uniformly. There are commercial heating blankets and large hot plates available. A hot box can be constructed easily from 2 × 4 framing. The heat source can be a hot air gun or household baseboard heater.

An existing boat or a male plug (lath type) should be used to form the PVC hull. Since the required heat is only about 200°F, there is no danger to the finish on the boat used for a form. However, a sheet of polyethylene should be used to cover the boat to prevent any resin from sticking when you start to glass. The PVC foam waxes or parting agents should not be used since

Fig. 10-36. Pouring up urethane foam in a sailboat mold.

they might prevent a good bond when glassing the inside of the hull. The sheets of PVC, after they are pliable, are draped over plug or form and butted. Any tailoring can be easily done with a *sloyd knife.* Pins, small dowels or wire lacing may be used to hold the sheets together. Any gaps between sheets should be filled with a mortar of resin and thixotropic powder such as *Cab-O-Sil* or small pieces of PVC foam. The hull can now be covered with fiber glass cloth. The weight of cloth and the number of layers will be determined by the size of the hull. The resin selected must be compatible with the type of PVC foam used.

Fabrication

Foamed *polystyrene (styrofoam)* is an ideal material for making masters and one-off models. It is a relatively soft, grainless material that can be readily carved or sanded. A *surform file* is

Fig. 10-37. Hollowing out a section with a foam cutter.

the ideal tool for shaping styrofoam. It may be purchased in slabs 20″ × 7″ × 9′. These slabs, when sliced into 20″ × 3-½″ × 9′ pieces, are ideal for use in construction of surfboards. Pieces may also be built up using epoxy resin. A hot wire cutter or electric carving knife make cutting styrofoam a breeze (Fig. 10-37).

Foamboard (*Monsanto*) consists of a ¼-inch styrofoam core covered with Kraft paper. It is inexpensive (about $3-$4 for a 40″ × 60″ sheet). It is an easy material to work with, and Kraft paper cover simplifies layout. By scoring the surface with a bone (used in leather craft and printing), the foam board can be bent or folded. This material does not have sufficient strength for full-scale applications, but it is ideal for large models.

Sheet cellular material lends itself to the design and fabrication of one-off models. The design of the finished structure will determine the type of cellular plastic sheet to use. Cellular plastics, like all plastics, are either thermoforming or thermosetting. If the shape being made has no compound curves, then a thermosetting plastic or thermoforming plastic can be used. If there are compound curves, then it is necessary to use a thermoforming plastic (PVC foam sheet).

In fabricating a small sailboat or dingy, without compound curves, a simple form is constructed with three or four frames and several stringers. The transom which acts as rear form should be from plywood if the boat is going to be powered. The sheet is then place-tacked to the form. Place a strip of scrap wood over the foam prior to nailing. Trim sheet plastic with a sharp knife. Any irregularities can be removed with a sanding block (Fig. 10-38). The same procedure is followed to apply the rest of the sheeting to the form. Dowels (1/16-inch) can be used to pin the sheets together. Don't worry about any small gaps where sheets meet. They can be filled with a mortar of resin and thixotropic powder or resin and milled glass fibers.

The hull should now be given a coat of catalized resin. After the resin has set, any small irregularities can be filled with body putty. The hull is now ready for glassing (Fig. 10-39). Local reinforcement of additional layers of glass should be applied where necessary.

CEMENTING ACRYLICS

Tough yet soft, stiff but flexible, easy to machine and simple to form, these plastics have about all the desirable qualities one could wish for in a single material. Even the most deeply colored will exhibit the sparkling transparency so characteristic of these plastics (Fig. 10-40).

Both Plexiglas and Lucite are available in sheets, rods, tubes, some special shapes and in an assortment of colors,

Fig. 10-38. Sanding a large model sailboat styrofoam blank.

113

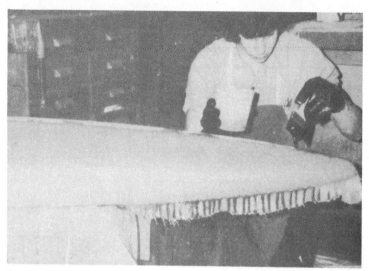

Fig. 10-39. Glassing a large model sailboat.

transparent, translucent and opaque. They can be sawed, filed, sanded, drilled, carved, turned, milled and polished with regular wood and metalworking tools and machines. Most fascinating is the very plasticity they possess when heated. You can tie a square knot in a heated rod as easily as in a hemp rope.

An ordinary baking oven can be used for heating since the temperature is kept fairly low—between 200-300°F. Too much heat causes permanent damage. On removing the plastic sheet from the oven, fan it through the air for a few seconds to chill and harden the surface. Then form it quickly. If it cools and stiffens before the forming is complete, it can be reheated and reformed. Wooden dies lined with billiard felt are used when several pieces are desired.

When cementing acrylics, the recommendations of the manufacturer should be followed, since it is a chemical process. *Glacial acetic acid* or *ethelene dichloride* are commonly used as solvent cements.

The soak method for cementing involves the dipping of one of the pieces into the solvent until a soft cushion is formed. Then it is pressed against the other piece and allowed to harden for three to five hours. The solvent can also be applied to the surfaces with a brush. The pieces are then pressed together to force out air bubbles. The joint usually hardens enough to allow further working in about 15 minutes.

114

Drive screws and selftapping screws are also used, especially when two different types of plastics are to be fastened together.

Polishing is done by using progressively fine abrasives until the final high gloss where a clean cloth buffing wheel is used. Acrylics polish so easily that one must be careful about overdoing it. They absorb heat from the buffer and tend to soften, so constant inspection is necessary.

VACUUM FORMING

Vacuum forming by hand with this simple, inexpensive equipment is a safe and exciting handcraft with less than a $50 investment. The process consists of heating a plastic sheet over an electric, gas, or charcoal heat source; manually pressing and sealing the heated sheet over a pattern onto a sturdy flat table; exhausting the remaining air under the sheet with a vacuum; and letting the formed piece cool, removing the pattern and trimming the finished piece. Scrap pieces as small as 3″ or 4″ square can be reheated and used for smaller projects.

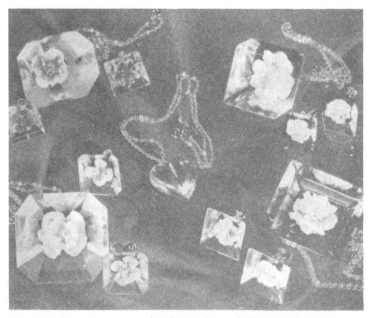

Fig. 10-40. Attractive costume jewelry can be made by internal carving.

Working Surface

A rigid, flat table 30" high is required. Most projects can be handled on a 48" × 30" table. The largest plastic sheet that is currently standard and easy to buy is 40" × 72" × 3/16". This could be handled on a 48" × 84" table. If a small table is built and a large project made, a 48" × 84" sheet of ¾" plywood could be evenly supported over two or more work benches. Making a table portable may be desirable, especially if the heat source is external to the work area.

Vacuum System

Building a good vacuum system is easily and inexpensively accomplished using scrap components. Although vacuum pumps are rarely seen in junk yards, old refrigerator compressors are abundant; some have motors. A one or two cylinder compressor should be selected which, when turned by hand, appears to have compression.

Drain the compressor and flush its refrigerant-contaminated crank case. Motor oil (SAE 30 or 40) added to the crank case should make up for any piston ring and cylinder wear. By hooking the compressor's intake to the vacuum reservoir tank, a vacuum pump will result. A ¼ to ¾ hp motor will be adequate.

When choosing an electric motor from a scrap yard, check the name plate for desired horsepower and voltage, see if the shaft turns and is not bent, sniff the motor to determine if it smells burned, and avoid capacitor-type motors. Most electric motors purchased by this method will work and not cost more than six cents per pound.

As a vacuum reservoir tank, a 30 gallon hot water tank, a hot water expansion tank, or a junk propane tank will be sufficient. To pull vacuum from the forming table to the reservoir tank, a ¾" pipe is needed with fittings and a gas cock.

A powerful vacuum cleaner's capacity in volume of air could make it more desirable for large formings. Although the vacuum cleaner doesn't create as high a vacuum as a piston pump, a large forming may not require high vacuum pressure. A vacuum cleaner also requires no recovery time.

Heat Source

Most small formings can be heated by an electric hot plate or range burner. The plastic sheet is handheld over the heat source and moved to distribute the heat to the desired areas.

116

With high-impact styrene, the formed area must be heated until it begins to sag and become rubber-like, with the outer perimeter heated until it becomes slightly ductile. The sheet is then placed over the pattern; a wooden frame is located over the sheet, pressed down, and held with hand pressure to form a seal.

For intermediate and large sheets, fasten the sheet to a wooden frame. Construction grade 1″ × 6″ lumber, with one edge joined flat, makes a good frame. The plastic sheet can be fastened to the holding frame with anything from carpet tacks to blue lath nails, depending on sheet thickness.

The frame with fastened sheet is next inverted and held over a heat source. The four burners of a 24″ or 30″ kitchen range can heat intermediate size sheets. Large size sheets are best heated over a charcoal or coke fire. The frames can be hand-held over the heat sources, or devices can be built to hold the frames. Rising heat is trapped by the walls of the frame. A modular charcoal heating unit is needed for every four or five square feet of sheet to be heated. The soft plastic acts as its own gasket.

Charcoal heating may seem primitive, but because of the large electrical power requirements (40,000 W) required to equal 10 pounds of burning charcoal, and the relative infrequency of using and storing such an electrical unit, charcoal is a very practical solution. To heat electrically on less power would require an oven-type unit which would take up too much space.

Forming Method

Vacuum forming with handheld methods is no different from vacuum forming with sophisticated equipment. The pattern should not be higher than it is wide. Avoid sharp corners, undercuts, and drawing into a cavity. One and one-half degrees is a good minimum for draught. Allow the plastic to heat and sag enough so it won't be overstretched by the vacuum process. Too much sag will cause the material to fold rather than stretch (Fig. 10-41).

A pattern placed over the vacuum hole of a table will need to be vented to prevent the hole from being blocked and allow the vacuum to reach around the pattern. Rip and cross-cut ⅛″ deep table-saw cuts on the bottom of the pattern. Half-inch square wire mesh placed under the pattern will serve as vents. When a pattern has a recess, vent by drilling a hole to the trapped area.

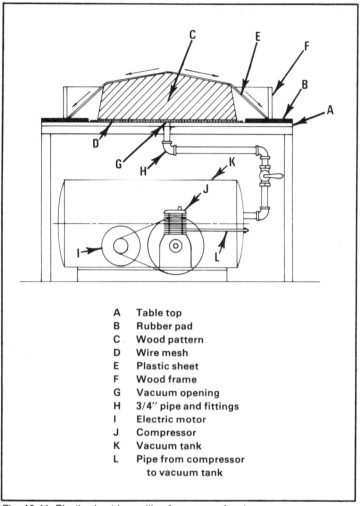

A	Table top
B	Rubber pad
C	Wood pattern
D	Wire mesh
E	Plastic sheet
F	Wood frame
G	Vacuum opening
H	3/4" pipe and fittings
I	Electric motor
J	Compressor
K	Vacuum tank
L	Pipe from compressor to vacuum tank

Fig. 10-41. Plastic sheet in position for vacuum forming.

When forming large sheets, use a firm closed-cell foam rubber mat as a gasket. Large sheets are often uneven in thickness, and the heads of nails holding the sheets to the frame make sealing directly to the table top difficult.

After the framed sheet has been positioned, the weight of as many people as possible is applied to press the frame into the rubber gasket pad before the vacuum valve is opened. Once the seal has been established and the vacuum is on, no hand pressure is needed.

Lightly dusting the heated sheet and the pattern with talcum powder will help the pattern part from the formed piece. In most cases it is best to bang the pattern out of the formed plastic before removing the nailed plastic sheet from the wood forming frame.

Rough trim the formed piece on a band saw. Fine trim can be done on a radial arm saw with the blade turned horizontal and protected, or a 3″ diameter saw blade mounted on a shaper with a roller arbor guide. It may be necessary to place the formed piece back on the pattern for positioning while trimming.

Underheated sheets can be salvaged by gently reheating. Overheated sheets are best laid on a flat table, allowed to cool, and then cut into usable sized pieces for other projects. Good sized pieces of trim can also be saved for reheating on small projects.

Machines and Equipment

This concluding chapter explains the construction of four devices that are often used when working with plastics. The equipment pieces or machine include an infrared oven, thermoforming machine, granulator, compression molder and vacuum forming units.

INFRARED OVEN

Hot-forming acrylic plastic normally requires the uniform heat of a thermostatically-regulated oven, either gas or electric. You can easily and inexpensively make an oven which, while not thermostatically controlled, is sufficient for hot-forming small pieces of acrylic plastic.

This homemade oven uses infrared heat to minimize the danger of overheating and charring the plastic. Infrared rays penetrate objects without first heating the surface, thus heating the objects from the inside out. Acrylic pieces more than an inch thick can be easily heated in this infrared oven. See table 11-1 for materials.

Construction, as illustrated by Figs. 11-1 through 11-3, is routinely simple. After the oven has been built, cut a 3"-diameter hole in the lid to accommodate an observation window. Form a convex window from a piece of clear acrylic ⅛" × 44" in diameter. Drill four evenly-spaced holes (⅛" diameter) around the circumference of the window opening and corresponding

Table 11-1. Materials List for the Infrared Oven.

Quantity	Part	Size
1	Steel waste can	20 gal.
4	Frosted infrared heat lamps	250w − 115-125v
1	Standard plug fuse	30 amp
1	Switch and fuse box w/switch	
4	Standard porcelain receptacles	
8 Ft.	Insulated wiring	No. 14
1	Lamp support base (plywood)	½″ × 10¾″ × 21″
1	Shelf (plywood)	½″ × 12″ × 21″
1	Asbestos sheet	¼″ × 12 ″ 21″
1	Switch and fuse box support (plywood)	¾″ × 4″ × 4″
1	Front support (plywood)	¾″ × 4½″ × 12″
1	Rear support (plywood)	¾″ × 5½″ × 12″
4	Metal cleats	16 gauge × ½″ × 2″
1	Window (acrylic)	⅛″ × 4½″ dia.
1	Butt hinge	2½″ × 2½″
3 Ft.	Sash chain	No. 8
1	Electrical pig tail	No. 14 − 6 Ft.
4	Wood screws	¾″ × No. 8 F.H.
8	Wood screws	1″ × No. 8 R.H.
4	Wood screws	½″ × No. 8 F.H.
22	Machine bolts w/nuts	⅛″ × ½″ R.H.

holes through the acrylic. The insertion and tightening of the machine bolts completes your oven. Begin baking.

THERMOFORMING MACHINE

Since the thermoforming process is widely used in industry, one important piece of equipment is a *thermoforming machine*. A thermoforming machine retails for about $900 but one which will perform vacuum operations on high-impact polystyrene up to .08″ thick can be built at a low cost. The machine can be adapted to perform blow and mechanical forming operations inexpensively.

Construction of a thermoforming machine is relatively simple (Fig. 11-4 through 11-6). Its general size is determined by the forming area desired, taking into consideration the sizes of available plastics. The critical areas are the clamping-frame opening, which should be about ¼″ smaller in each direction

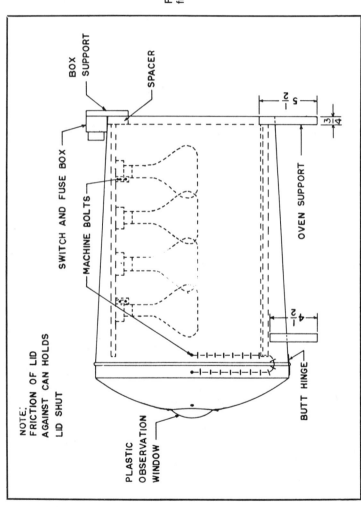

Fig. 11-1. Side view detail of the infrared oven.

122

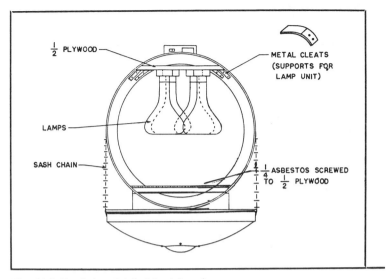

Fig. 11-2. Front view detail of the infrared oven.

than the cut plastics, and the mold-forming base which should be about ⅛″ smaller in each direction than the clamping-frame opening. A shop vacuum is used as the machine's vacuum source.

To use the vacuum thermoforming machine, a mold is placed on the forming base, and the softened plastic, while held

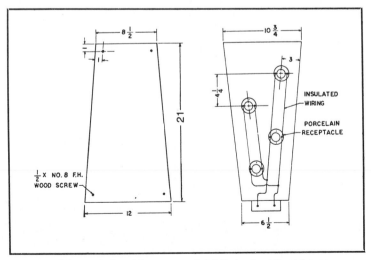

Fig. 11-3. Bottom shelf and lamp support details for the infrared oven.

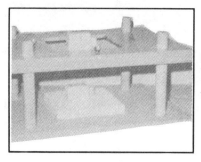

Fig. 11-4. A mold is placed on the forming base. The softened plastic, while held in the clamping frames, is forced against the mold.

in the clamping frames, is forced against the mold as shown in Fig. 11-4. The vacuum is applied, and the plastic sheet then takes the shape of the mold. Figure 11-5 shows the mold and formed plastic removed. The plastic sheet can be softened by holding it in the clamping frame over a heat source, or by placing the entire unit in an oven.

GRANULATOR

Don't let budget problems keep you from enjoying the benefits of having a granulator (Fig. 11-7). A granulator offers a number of advantages, particularly if you are working with thermoplastic material. There is little need to buy granulated thermoplastic material for processing. Also, many of the thermoplastics are available in the form of disposable type items, worn out products or trimmings from thermoforming. Purchase of a comparable variety of plastic materials in small quantities is often difficult and usually expensive.

While thermoplastics are commonly recycled, various thermosets also can be reground and used in somewhat different ways. For example, RTV silicone, recycled from molds which have been damaged, improperly lost, or have served their initial purpose,

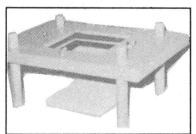

Fig. 11-5. This view shows the mold and formed plastic removed.

makes and ideal filler when mixed with liquid silicone to produce new molds. Using the reground RTV material is a significant savings.

A granulator grinds pieces of plastic material which are small enough to drop through a hopper into a cutterhead rotated either by direct or belt drive. Cutterhead knives pass within about .005 inch of a stationary knife which shears the material until it can pass through a screen of predetermined size, usually 3/16 to ⅜ inch. The granulate is then collected for further processing.

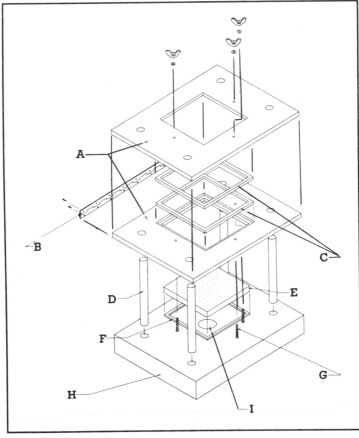

Fig. 11-6. Parts for the thermoforming machine. (A) Clamping frame: ½" plywood. (B) Piano hinge. (C) Sponge rubber weatherstripping; ¼" × ⅜" flush fitting with clamping frame. (D) Clamping frame guides: 1" wood dowel. (E) Mold forming base: ½" plywood, ⅛" holes. (F) Forming base riser: ⅛" × ¼" wood. (G) Stove bolts: ¼" × 1¼". (H) Platen: 3⅜" plywood. (I) Vacuum receptacle.

Fig. 11-7. A plastics granulator offers advantages when working with thermo-plastic material.

A granulator can be constructed with a welder, drill press, band saw and hand tools. Standard, commercially available items are used whenever possible. These include: motor, cutterhead, pulleys, belts and switches. Most of the parts can be surplus or salvaged. The cost of all purchased parts is under $25. See Fig. 11-8.

The design centers around an 8-inch Powermatic jointer head, with bearings and bearing blocks, which become the cutterhead. A 4- or 6-inch cutterhead can be used with proportional reduction in dimensions, horsepower, and cost. A permanent screen and housing for the cutterhead is made from a 10-inch section of 3½-inch inside diameter black iron pipe. Holes are countersunk on the outside to increase clearance for the granulated material passing through. A slightly coarser granulate, satisfactory for injection molding, can be produced with ¼-inch holes. This will also result in faster granulating.

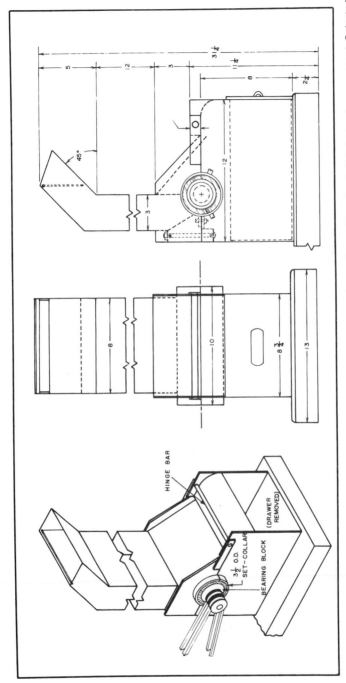

Fig. 11-8. The cabinet is 3/16" sheet steel with weld seams. The hopper is hinged to the base with a simple ½" steel rod arrangement. Selected dimensions of views are provided as a guide.

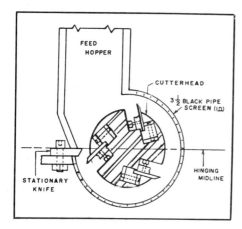

Fig. 11-9. Detail of cutter section.

The pipe is cut in half lengthwise and a quarter section is cut from one of the halves to allow the material to feed into the cutterhead from the hopper (Fig. 11-9). The cutterhead is mounted in the lower half of the pipe with 3½-inch outside diameter set-collars which have an inside diameter to fit the cutterhead bearing blocks. The lower assembly is fastened with machine screws.

The upper screen (pipe) is welded to the hopper section, and the lower half to the base section, which is bolted to plywood (Fig.

Fig. 11-10. By opening the hopper section, the cutterhead, stationary knife and screen are readily accessible for adjustment and cleaning.

11-10). The stationary knife is made from 1018 crs ¼ by 1½ inches. properly hardened, the 1018 steel will produce a Rockwell hardness of C-45. A higher carbon steel may be desirable for greater hardness. The knife is bolted in place with approximately .003 clearance between it and the cutterhead knives. The collection bin is made of wood because of the ease of construction and to reduce noise from vibration.

A 2-hp, 1160 rpm motor provides the power (as little as 1 hp can be used for smaller units). A pulley ratio of 1:2 produces a cutterhead speed of about 2320 rpm. Slower speeds are often effective. Twin V-belts can be used for greater efficiency. For maximum saftey a magnetic switch is installed on the main power control.

COMPRESSION MOLDER

A simple compression molder can be built for about $10 to $12. The unit described here can handle various size molds up to 6 inches high by 8 inches square (Fig. 11-11). It has a material capacity of approximately five to 10 ounces. The machine can be made entirely of wood. It uses a concentric cam for leverage and various shimming devices to accommodate different mold sizes.

As a result of this simple leverage process, many tons of pressure can be achieved which enables you to produce a wide range of products including dinnerware, air scoops for vehicles and water sleds. Molds can be made from *hydrostone* and simple tooling jell coat resin for about 65 cents per matched mold. Simple release agents such as wax, fatty acids and polyvinyl alcohol provide excellent surface finishes for the products.

Fig. 11-11. This low-cost molder develops tons of pressure.

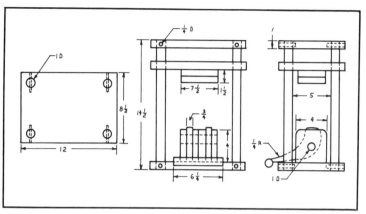

Fig. 11-12. Construction details for the compression molder.

How to Make It

Begin the molder by cutting three 8 ½ by 12-inch platens from 1-inch plywood. Bore 1-inch holes in the corners of each platen. Cut four pieces of 1-inch dowel, 14 ½-inches long. Position the dowels through the three platens. Drill ¼-inch holes in the corners of the top and bottom platens, 2 ½-inches deep, for the locking dowels. Cut to length eight ¼-inch locking dowels, apply glue and push into position. See Fig. 11-12.

Cut two pieces of birch ¾ by 4 by 7 ½ inches to be used for the shim which is attached to the bottom of the middle platen. Locate the shim in the center of the platen, drill holes and attach with screws.

Fabricating the Cam

The cam assembly must be constructed of hardwood. Cut four pieces of birch ¾ by 4 by 4 inches to be used for the cam lock. Cut two pieces of birch, ¾ by 4 by 6 inches to be used for cams. Lay out cams on the material and cut to size. Bore ½-inch holes in the end of each cam for attaching the handle. Bore 1-inch holes through each piece of the cam lock and through the two cams. Cut a piece of 1-inch dowel, 4 ½-inches long, and fit it into the cams and the pieces used for locking. Align the assembly and place the dowel through the assembly.

Cut a 6 ¼-inch piece of 1-inch dowel for the handle and drill two ½-inch holes for dowel attachment to the handle. Cut two ½-inch dowels, 2 ½-inches long, apply glue and assemble the handle to the cams.

130

Locate the complete cam assembly on the bottom platen and determine the position of the screws for attachment to the platen. Drill holes and attach assembly with screws. Sand and finish the molder.

BUILDING AND OPERATING A VACUUM FORMING UNIT

Vacuum forming of plastics makes possible fabrication of a large number of useful projects. It also permits a considerable reduction of project costs because of its suitability for low-cost plastic material. In many instances, however, the cost of the vacuum-forming machine prohibits this technique of plastic work. For approximately $25, plus some interesting work, you can construct the vacuum-forming unit in Fig. 11-13. The vacuum pump is the only additional item required.

This unit operates on the same basis as larger industrial machines. It enables you to learn about a widely used method of plastic forming; possible uses for vacuum-formed articles; heating, forming, and assembly techniques; and some of the scientific principles necessary for its operation.

The unit has been designed for use with 10″ × 14⅜″ sheets of high-impact polystyrene which allows a minimum of waste from a standard-sized (40″ × 72″) sheet. Sheet thicknesses of .040″, .060″ and .080″ have been used for the projects illustrated (Fig. 11-14).

Fig. 11-13. The completed vacuum forming unit.

Fig. 11-14. Samples of the kinds of things that can be made when using the vacuum forming unit.

The three basic parts of the unit are: the heater, vacuum chamber and clamp mechanism. The purpose of the heater is to soften the plastic sheet to a condition for vacuum forming. It would be possible to eliminate the heater if some other heat source, such as a plastics heating oven, were available. However, this would require that the clamp mechanism be handled with gloves because it would need to be placed in the oven also. When using the heater, clamp temperatures are not high enough to burn the hands.

The clamp mechanism consists of an upper and lower clamp with bolts and wing nuts which hold the sheet plastic in place during heating and forming. Attached also are pressure strips and clamps which prevent air leaks between the sheet plastic and the vacuum chamber.

The vacuum chamber holds the patterns and permits the air evacuation between them and the plastic sheet. Patterns can be replaced in a matter of minutes by simply removing four screws and then replacing them with a new pettern plate and set of patterns. The vacuum tank shown was adapted from an old fire extinguisher, but it is not a necessity. However, it does permit a more controlled rate of evacuation which is necessary on deep draws and crowded patterns where webbing is likely to occur.

Construction of the vacuum-forming unit is quite simple. Most of the required materials, except the toggle clamps, can be obtained locally.

Heater Assembly

Cut the components shown in table 11-2 and Fig. 11-15 to size. Construct the heating element from a ¼" diameter coil of #20 nichrome, measured to approximately 800 w. Place one end of the coil in a vise and stretch one-half of it to a length of 36". Stretch the other end of the coil to a 60" length . The more tightly wound 36" coil will be used for the outside of the element pattern where more heat is necessary.

Place ½" × 4-40 roundhead machine screws in each of the binding-post holes and hold in place with a nut. Carefully wind the element according to the pattern and secure to the binding posts with a second nut (Figs. 11-16 and 11-17). Attach an asbestos-covered heater cord to the element from the bottom side of the heater base.

Assemble the sides, ends, corners and heater base supports. Trim the heater to fit if necessary, and fasten it to the heater supports with ½" × 4-40 roundhead machine screws (Fig. 11-16).

Vacuum Chamber

Construct the vacuum chamber base from a close-grained wood. Saw ⅛" deep grooves, approximately ¾" from the ends and

Table 11-2. Materials Needed for the Parts Shown in Fig. 11-15.

Part	Item	Material	Size
A	Pressure bar	Angle iron (⅛ × ¾ × ¾)	7
B	Vacuum-chamber top	Hardbound	¼ × 9⅜ × 13¾
C	Vacuum-chamber base	Wood	¾ × 9⅜ × 13¾
D	Vacuum-chamber seal	Hardboard	¼ × 9⅜ × 13¾
E	Vent tube	⅛ Long Nipple-3	⅛
F	Pattern plate	Hardboard	¼ × 8 1/16 × 12 7/16
G	Vent grooves		⅛ × ⅛
H	Pressure clamp (location shown only)	Danly Toggle Clamp	#9-00-19
I	Upper clamp	Angle iron (⅛ × 1½ × 1½)	12½ × 16⅞
J	Lower clamp	Angle iron (⅛ × 1½ × 1½)	12 × 16⅜
K	Pressure strip	Sponge-rubber weather strip	3/16 × ⅜
L	Clamp bolts	Stove bolts and wing nuts	¼ × ¾ fh
M	Corner	Angle iron (⅛ × 1½ × 1½)	6 (before bending)
N	End	Asbestos cement board	¼ × 4½ × 9½
O	Side	Asbestos cement board	¼ × 4½ × 13⅜
P	Heater base	Asbestos cement board	¼ × 9 × 13⅜
Q	Heating element	Nichrome—800w	¼ coil— #20 wire
R	Heater-base side support	Angle iron (⅛ × ¾ × ¾)	13⅜
S	Heater-base end support	Angle iron (⅛ × ¾ × ¾)	7½

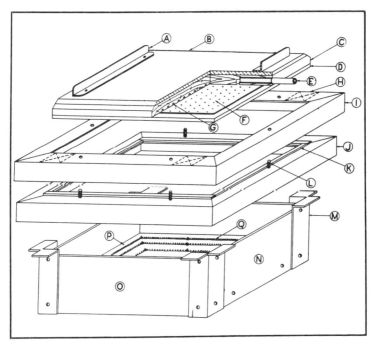

Fig. 11-15. Parts of the vacuum forming unit.

edges, with a circular saw. The remaining grooves should be spaced ½″ apart with three crosswise grooves cut approximately as shown in Fig 11-18. Drill a 25/64″ hole 3½″ from the edge for the vent tube.

Mark ⅝″ back from the edges of the vacuum-chamber seal and cut out the center area with a fine scroll-saw blade. Save the center for use as the pattern plate.

Glue the vacuum chamber top, base, and seal together, keeping the smooth side of the hardboard out. When dry, chamfer the top edges ½″ to allow clearance for the pressure clamps.

Drill 1/16″ vent holes in the pattern plate according to the shape of the pattern. Space the vent holes about ½″ apart and as close to the pattern as possible. The holes need not line up with the vent grooves because the rough bottom surface of the hardboard will allow air passage. Fasten the pattern plate to the base with flathead wood screws where convenient.

Apply several coats of lacquer or shellac to the ends and edges of the wood base to seal the pores and prevent air leakage. Do not attach the pressure bars until the proper location can be determined with the pressure clamps.

Clamp Mechanism

Cut material for the clamps according to sizes shown in Table 11-2. Weld the lower clamp on the inside, making certain that the top face remains level. Drill and countersink holes for the clamp bolts, but do not weld in position until after the holes for the upper clamp have been drilled. Weld the upper clamp on the inside corner and top face, making certain that the inside face remains level. Center the upper clamp over the lower clamp, and drill holes for the clamp bolts accordingly. Locate the pressure clamps 2″ from each end. Drill and countersink holes for ¾″ × 10-24 flathead machine screws. Shims of ¼″ hardboard must be placed under the clamps before fastening them in place.

The pressure bars can now be placed in position on the vacuum chamber by the following procedure:

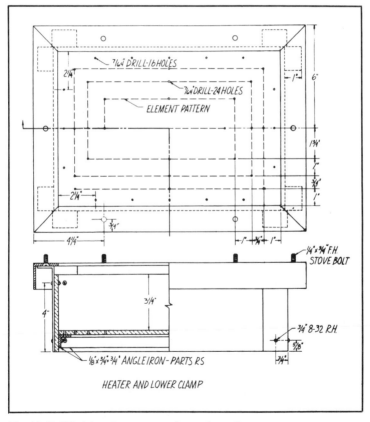

Fig. 11-16. Wind the element according to the pattern.

Fig. 11-17. View of the heating element.

● Adhere the pressure strip around the inside edge of the lower clamp.

● Place a plastic sheet in position and attach the upper clamp.

● Place the vacuum chamber (without pattern plate) in position.

● Place the pressure bars under the pressure clamps. If the clamp does not close tightly, a shim will be necessary under the pressure bar.

● Test with a vacuum pump to see if any leaks exist. In proper operation, the plastic sheet will bend into the space for-

Fig. 11-18. Remaining grooves should be spaced ½" apart with three crosswise grooves cut approximately as shown.

merly occupied by the pattern plate and will remain there for a moment without additional pumping. Additional shims for more clamping pressure might be necessary. Fasten the pressure bars in position when the vacuum chamber seals correctly.

Paint the outside of the heater and the clamps with heat-resistant aluminum paint. Attach the heater to a plywood base with corner brackets. A switch box should be conveniently placed in front of the heater to control the vacuum pump and heating element. If a vacuum tank is available, place it close to the heater assembly as shown in Fig. 11-19.

Patterns

Wood patterns have been used for most of the projects made, but any strong material or usable object, which can withstand the temporary heat of the sheet plastic, is suitable. As a general rule for good forming, the depth of the pattern should not exceed more than one-half of its width. A 3½" maximum should be the maximum depth of the die.

Operating Procedure

● Place the clamp mechanism over the heater and preheat until the clamps warm slightly. Cold clamps will absorb heat from the edges of the plastic and prevent good forming.

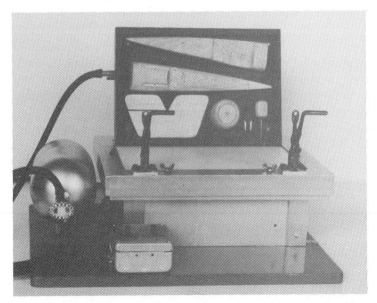

Fig. 11-19. If a vacuum tank is available, place it close to the heater assembly.

137

Fig. 11-20. A simple box-like design marks the machine, powered by a vacuum cleaner and heated by a standard clothes iron.

- Place a sheet of plastic between the upper and lower clamps and tighten the wing nuts.
- Heat the plastic sheet for 3 to 4 minutes, depending on the thickness.
- Clamp the vacuum chamber and patterns in place with the pressure clamps.
- Evacuate the air between the vacuum chamber and the plastic sheet. Remove the vacuum chamber and clamps from the heater and allow to cool. It is often advisable to turn over the clamp and vacuum chamber to observe the process and control the rate of evacuation.

Vacuum-formed projects can be worked and finished using many of the same techniques as for other plastic materials. With a little experimentation and practice, many vacuum-formed projects will be possible. The types of projects are restricted only to the limitations of the forming process and your ingenuity.

VACUUM CLEANER-POWERED VACUUM FORMING MACHINE

A simple vacuum-forming machine can be built using an ordinary electric clothes iron as a source of heat and a household vacuum cleaner to create the necessary vacuum (Fig. 11-20). The plastic material to be formed can be cut from the sides of a liquid bleach bottle (Fig. 11-21).

Construction

The machine is essentially a small box made of ¾" plywood with inside dimensions of 4" long, 3½" wide and 4" deep. The sides are fastened with screws and glue, and care should be taken to make all joints airtight.

Inside the box, about ½" from the top, is a heavy sheet of aluminium about 1/16" thick. This sheet is deeply scribed in a cross-hatch pattern to allow for the escape of air, for reasons to be described later. Hardboard, with the rough side up, also works very well.

The sheet of aluminum is properly supported by two cut-to-fit hardboard spacers (Fig. 11-22). Around the top of the box, four pieces of ⅛" × ¾" band iron are held down by nuts turned onto 3/16" × 1½" hanger bolts. These four pieces of band iron hold the plastic in place during the forming process. In one end of the box a hole is bored for a pipe nipple to be threaded tightly into the box. The diameter of the pipe nipple depends on the diameter of the vacuum hose that will be connected to it.

Fig. 11-21. Raw materials to be processed by the machine are cut from the type of liquid bleach bottle shown here.

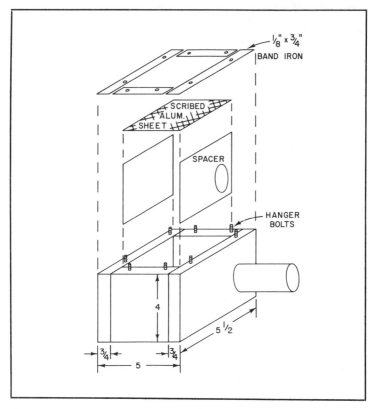

Fig. 11-22. Construction details for the simple vacuum forming machine.

In most cases, items up to 4″ thick may be vacuum formed with this machine. Following is the step-by-step procedure for its use.

● Adjust the height of the scribed aluminum sheet by using longer or shorter hardboard spacers. The highest point of the pattern should be at least ⅛″ below the top edge of the box to allow for sag in the heated plastic.

● Place the pattern in the center of the aluminum sheet.

● Cut a piece of plastic, 4″ × 4½″, from the side of a plastic bleach bottle and place it on top of the box.

● Put the pieces of band iron in place on the plastic and fasten them down securely with the nuts.

● Slip the vacuum hose over the pipe nipple.

● Place the electric clothes iron on top of the box so that it rests on the nuts.

● Turn the heat selector of the iron to its highest temperature.

● After a short time, depending on the heat of the iron, the plastic will begin to expand and buckle. Continue applying heat to the plastic until it takes on a glossy appearance. The plastic will also sag slightly at this time. If the plastic takes on a brown, scorched appearance, it has been overheated.

● As soon as the plastic looks glossy across its entire surface, turn on the vacuum and remove the electric iron. The plastic will be drawn over the pattern as the air is evacuated through the scribe lines on the aluminum sheet, past the edges of the aluminum sheet, past the edges of the aluminum sheet, and into the box.

● Allow the plastic to cool several minutes before removing it from the machine. If you encounter difficulty in removing the pattern from the plastic, dust the pattern with some type of dusting powder before each use. Portland cement works very well in such instances.

Index

Edited by Robert E. Ostrander